2001

Personal Prayer Journal

WORLD WIDE PUBLICATIONS
Minneapolis, Minnesota 55403

The Importance of Prayer

Prayer is our most important work as Christians. It is a journey filled with the satisfaction of helping the helpless, and of seeing the purposes of God fulfilled and the strategies of Satan thwarted. In the unseen arena of prayer the real work of God is forged. We often see the results in the visible world, but God is moving behind the scenes, acting in response to those who labor daily in prayer.

Exodus 17 illustrates this principle vividly. As the Israelite army fought the Amalekites on the plain of Rephidim, Moses stood on a hill overlooking the battle. Whenever he held up the staff of God, Israel prevailed. But when he lowered the staff, the Amalekites gained the advantage. A clear principle of prayer emerges from this account: God acts in response to the prayers of his intercessors, supernaturally enabling those he has called to accomplish the assigned task. Moses' part in the victory, though probably unseen and unnoticed by those in the fight, was vital.

Our role in the work of God throughout the world may be unnoticed, unseen, unappreciated. But, like Moses, God calls us to "hold up the staff of God"—to pray. In fact, God is looking "for a man among them who would build up the wall and stand before me in the gap on behalf of the land so I would not have to destroy it, but I found none" (Ezekiel 22:30). We need to take our part in the plan and program of God seriously, developing the attitude that Samuel had toward Israel when he said, "As for me, far be it from me that I should sin against the Lord by failing to pray for you" (1 Samuel 12:23).

Prayer is work. Prayer is hard work. But prayer is a holy work as well—vital and indispensable. God has a more difficult time finding people for *prayer* than he does for any other assignment.

THE PERSONAL PRAYER JOURNAL IS DESIGNED

1. To provide practical insights from God's Word on prayer.

2. To provide a suggested plan for a prayer ministry that is manageable, measurable, and useful.
3. To provide the means of making prayer ministry a reality.

In order to make a tool like the *Personal Prayer Journal* work, we need the determination to be faithful to the commitment.

1. Our primary responsibility is to be faithful to pray. The results of our prayers are God's responsibility.
2. We need to be realistic in our prayer ministry. Faithfulness to a short, daily prayer time is more desirable than occasional faithfulness to an unrealistic larger time commitment.
3. We should make daily entries of significant prayer items in the space provided on the calendar pages. These will become a source of tremendous encouragement and motivation as we look back at the written record of how God answered specific prayers.
4. The *Personal Prayer Journal* is designed for only one aspect of our spiritual life—prayer. We must not neglect regular reading and meditation in God's Word.

Principles of Prayer

As we begin to develop a personal prayer strategy, we need to examine some principles of prayer from God's Word. Three vital aspects of prayer are Attitudes in prayer, Obstacles to prayer, Answers to prayer.

ATTITUDES IN PRAYER

Prayer is conversation with God. But when we talk with God it is not just like any other conversation. There are several qualities that should mark our attitudes as we converse with our Creator:

Awe. When John the apostle saw the glorified Christ, he "fell at his feet as though dead" (Revelation 1:17). When the prophet Isaiah had his vision of the throne room of God, he exclaimed, "Woe to me! . . . I am ruined! For I am a man of unclean lips, and I live among a people of unclean lips, and my eyes have seen the King, the Lord Almighty" (Isaiah 6:5).

Yet, as A. W. Tozer has said,

We go to God as we send a boy to a grocery store with a long written list, "God, give me this," and our gracious God often gives us what we want. But I think God is disappointed because we make him no more than a source of what we want.

Awe simply means being constantly amazed at who God is and that he would even allow us to address him as "Father."

Helplessness. We must be genuinely convinced of our own inability to accomplish the thing for which we are praying to God. O. Hallesby, in his classic book, *Prayer,* highlights this truth when he says:

Be not anxious because of your helplessness. Above all, do not let it prevent you from praying. Helplessness is the real secret and the impelling power of prayer. You should therefore

rather try to thank God for the feeling of helplessness which He has given you. It is one of the greatest gifts which God can impart to us. For it is only when we are helpless *that we open our hearts to Jesus and let Him help us in our distress, according to His grace and mercy.*

The apostle Paul similarly speaks of our total inability to accomplish anything on our own in the spiritual realm. He confesses, "You see, at just the right time, when we were still powerless, Christ died for the ungodly" (Romans 5:6). And again in Romans 8:26 he says, "The Spirit helps us in our weakness. We do not know what we ought to pray for."

The proper starting place in prayer, then, is an awe of God, which in turn makes us see our own helplessness. It is the realization that we are totally powerless within ourselves to make our prayers happen. Our helplessness induces prayer.

Faith. But it takes more than helplessness. It is faith that shapes the cries of our hearts into genuine prayer. Hallesby points out that

Without faith there can be no prayer, no matter how great our helplessness may be. Helplessness united with faith produces prayer. Without faith our helplessness would only be a vain cry of distress in the night.

The writer of Hebrews agrees:

And without faith it is impossible to please God, because anyone who comes to him must believe that he exists and that he rewards those who earnestly seek him (11:6).

But faith is often the very thing we feel that we lack in our prayer life. Perhaps we do not understand that in the very act of praying we are demonstrating faith. By going to God, we exercise genuine faith. It may be a young faith, but it *is* faith! We have "faith enough" when we turn to Jesus in our helplessness. The *results* of prayer are the concern of God. *Our* concern is to come to him in prayer with the awareness that we are helpless in ourselves.

Confidence. The essence of faith is our confidence in God's ability to do what he has promised. Abraham stands as our clearest illustration of confident faith:

Yet he did not waver through unbelief regarding the promise of God, but was strengthened in his faith and gave glory to God, being fully persuaded that God had power to do what he had promised (Romans 4:20–21).

Too often we unconsciously shift our faith from confidence in God's ability to do what he has promised, to confidence in our ability to believe he will do a certain thing. In other words, we put our confidence in our faith rather than in God! Jesus makes it clear that the *size* of our faith is not what matters when he says, "I tell you the truth, if you have faith as small as a mustard seed, you can say to this mountain, 'Move from here to there' and it will move. Nothing will be impossible for you" (Matthew 17:20). It is the *object* of our faith—God—that is the basis of our confidence in prayer.

Persistence. In Matthew 7:7 Jesus says, "Ask and it will be given to you; seek and you will find; knock and the door will be opened to you." This verse translated literally says, "Ask and keep on asking . . . seek and keep on seeking . . . knock and keep on knocking." It shows us the importance of persistent prayer, of continuing to bring our prayers to God. Even Jesus, on the night of his betrayal, brought his anguished plea to the Father three times before relenting.

OBSTACLES TO PRAYER

Even the most mature Christians will sometimes feel that their prayers are not getting "beyond the ceiling." There are several things that can seriously hinder our prayer life:

Unconfessed Sin. David confessed, "If I had cherished sin in my heart, the Lord would not have listened" (Psalm 66:18). Isaiah tells us, "Surely the arm of the Lord is not too short to save, nor his ear too dull to hear. But your iniquities have separated you from your God; your sins have hidden his face from you, so that he will not hear" (Isaiah 59:1–2).

Sin renders our prayers useless because it alienates us from the object of our prayers—God. When we are out of fellowship with God due to unconfessed sin in our lives, our prayers are powerless monologues. We need to confess our sins of anger, lust, envy, gossip, or whatever else that has become a barrier between us and our Father. The basis of our access in prayer is fellowship with God.

Broken Fellowship with Others. Too often, "fellowship" is mistakenly understood to be an activity, when in fact it is a condition. Fellowship is not so much something we do as something we are either in or out of. The apostle John illuminates this for us:

> *If we claim to have fellowship with him yet walk in the darkness, we lie and do not live by the truth. But if we walk in the light, as he is in the light, we have fellowship with one another, and the blood of Jesus, his Son, purifies us from all sin (1 John 1:6–7).*

It is clear from this passage that our relationship with God is inseparably linked to our relationship with other believers. We cannot go to God in prayer when we are out of fellowship with one of his other children. Jesus emphasized this truth to his disciples in the Sermon on the Mount when he said:

> *Therefore, if you are offering your gift at the altar and there remember that your brother has something against you, leave your gift there in front of the altar. First go and be reconciled to your brother; then come and offer your gift (Matthew 5:23–24).*

Restitution of broken relationships is a prerequisite to effective prayer. This principle applies to relationships both inside and outside the church; it is especially relevant within the home. The apostle Peter said that conflict between spouses will "hinder" their prayers (1 Peter 3:7).

We can safely say in the light of these Scriptures that if we are not on speaking terms with God's people, we are not on speaking terms with God either. As with unconfessed sin in general, we should make immediate efforts to restore any broken relationship before we resume the ministry of intercession. If restoration is not possible immediately, we need to confess this broken fellowship to God and make a commitment to *him* to deal with it as soon as possible.

Wrong Motives. A final obstacle to prayer has to do with the intention of our hearts. James warns us,

When you ask, you do not receive, because you ask with wrong motives, that you may spend what you get on your pleasures (James 4:3).

If we pray for things that will feed that part of us known as our "sinful nature" (Romans 7:18), we cannot expect those prayers to reach the heart of God. Why not? Because God's goal for each one of us is to transform us into the likeness of his Son, Jesus Christ (Romans 8:29). God is not pleased to hear prayer that is contrary to his plans and purposes for our lives. But John assures us that we will be heard when we pray according to his will (1 John 5:14–15).

Our motives, the driving force behind our requests, are crucial factors that can limit the effectiveness of prayer.

ANSWERS TO PRAYER

God has promised to answer our prayers. Yet we need to understand the various forms an answer to prayer can assume. God's answers may sometimes be either a simple "yes" or "no." At other times, the answer may be more complex. The following are four possible ways that God may answer our prayers:

Request Granted. God's Word contains a multitude of promises that we will receive what we ask God for. This is especially true if we pray according to God's specific will for our lives—those things that he wants for us (1 John 5:14–15). Sometimes we pray specifically and God answers specifically. This is a marvelous experience, one that easily fosters courage and motivation for further prayer.

Request Granted, but not yet. Isaiah 55:8–9 instructs us that God's thoughts and methods are "higher" than ours—"as the heavens are higher than the earth." Sometimes God's timetable is different from ours! God's answer to our prayers in this case is indeed yes, but we must yield to his schedule. This is an answer, and it is an affirmative answer, but we can easily miss seeing the answer, or believe that God hasn't heard us, simply because the answer hasn't arrived on time. Patience and persistence in prayer are sometimes needed to ensure that we keep looking for God's answer.

Request Granted, but look elsewhere. At Jesus' final meal with his disciples, the night of his betrayal, he began to wash their feet (John 13:1–10). Peter was quite offended and when he tried to stop our Lord, Jesus told him that his perspective was wrong (vv. 6–7). Peter was looking so hard for what he expected to see (a conquering Messiah), that he failed to see what was there (a servant Messiah). There are times in prayer when we make a request, fully convinced of what form the answer will take. If God then answers in an unexpected fashion, we may fail to see the answer. We, like Peter, have our minds so made up about what should happen, we fail to see what is actually happening. We need to guard ourselves from unconsciously dictating how God will answer. We must give him the liberty to be God!

Request denied. In our relationship with God, sometimes a gradual but serious shift occurs in our own minds regarding who serves whom. Christians can easily forget that God is not a magic genie who jumps at every command. God is God. He is always at liberty to say no to our requests—not capriciously or maliciously, of course, for that would be a denial of his character. But he is still Lord of all. Times will come in our lives when God will deliberately withhold granting requests because of their ultimate effect on our lives or the lives of others. Perhaps the development of certain character qualities in our lives is more vital than the request sought. Withholding answers to prayer must always be understood as his ultimate *protection,* never as *punishment.* Our responsibility during these times of painful denial is to trust in what we know of God's love for us.

The Practice of Prayer

Without this final section, all that has been previously said is merely lifeless information. Talking about prayer is not prayer. To pray effectively, we need to know when, with whom, how, and what to pray.

WHEN TO PRAY

David prayed faithfully in the morning, evening, and often at noon (Psalm 5:3 and 55:17). Our Lord also spent times in prayer during early morning hours and late at night (Mark 1:35 and 6:46 ff.). Much can be said for "opening and closing" each day in communion with God. Often these times provide the most privacy and greatest freedom to be reflective and quiet.

Abraham's chief servant, sent by his master to secure a bride for Isaac, communed with God in the midst of a busy schedule, surrounded by strangers (Genesis 24:11–14). He prayed quietly in his heart (v. 45) in the midst of his work. It is acceptable and advisable to pray throughout the day as well as in the morning and evening. We need not be in the privacy of our homes to seek the face of God. Often, the Lord will bring to mind a person or an issue at the "oddest time." We need to seize these moments and use them to offer short, specific prayers back to God. Learning to respond to the unexpected promptings of the Holy Spirit is vital to a vibrant prayer life.

It is good to have a set time of daily prayer, but it is also important to seize the "eternal moments" that God gives throughout each day.

WITH WHOM TO PRAY

Jesus exhorts us to shun praying in public in order to impress others, and encourages us to pray "in secret" (Matthew 6:5–6). Private prayer will undoubtedly occupy the largest portion of our total prayer life. During these moments of solitude we can unveil our hearts before him who sees us as we are and yet loves us with an everlasting love. During these private hours we can intercede for the world that exists outside our private place. Here we can plead, weep, or rejoice over issues that matter little to anyone but us and God. Private prayer should be a priority.

But Jesus also speaks of praying with "two or three" (Matthew 18:19–20). The early Christians prayed together often (Acts 4:23–24; 12:12). A sweetness of fellowship and a sense of strength come when God's people go to him together in prayer.

God's Word holds before us models of private and corporate prayer; both are vital and should have a place in our prayer life.

HOW TO PRAY

It is more important *that* we pray than *how* we pray. Those who pray best are those who pray most. Yet, for some, a very broad format, a sort of "skeleton" model onto which personal detail can be added, is helpful.

A model for how to pray is captured in the acrostic: ACTS. Each letter stands for a specific aspect of prayer, arranged in a very natural order:

A— Adoration (worship)

C— Confession (of specific sins)

T— Thanksgiving (gratitude)

S— Supplication (specific requests)

Adoration. Worship begins and ends with who God is. Beginning our prayer time with adoration immediately places us in the position of a creature in the presence of its Creator. Adoration is simply acknowledging to God what he has revealed about himself. One helpful way to cultivate an attitude of adoration is to take actual phrases from Scripture and "pray them back" to God, using them as springboards of thought on who God is and what he is like. Some of the many appropriate passages for this purpose are Job 38; 1 Chronicles 29:10–13; Psalm 19:1–2; Psalm 84; Psalm 95:1–7; and many other Psalms.

Not only is this the proper starting place for prayer, it is a crucial driving force in our entire Christian life. As we worship, we must be sure that the One we worship is indeed the living God.

Confession. The closer we draw to God himself, the more we sense our own sinfulness. Again like Isaiah, a glimpse of God's glory will cause us to exclaim, "Woe to me" (Isaiah 6:5), as we realize how far we fall short of his glory.

The natural consequence of genuine adoration is sincere confession. It is reasonable that as we worship God, the awareness of our personal sin becomes greater.

Confession is the second step in prayer: agreeing with God that specific conduct and attitudes in our lives are wrong. We should name the sin and ask God to forgive us. During this period of confession, we may also ask God to make us aware of other sins in our life that we are unaware of or have neglected to deal with.

Thanksgiving. Our immediate response after confession is thanksgiving. David said, "Blessed is he whose transgressions are forgiven" (Psalm 32:1). We can certainly thank God for forgiving us of the sins we have just confessed. But gratitude to God should encompass more than forgiveness. Paul told the Colossians,

And whatever you do, whether in word or deed, do it all in the name of the Lord Jesus, giving thanks to God the Father through him (Colossians 3:17).

Thanksgiving causes us to acknowledge God's existence, his love, and his care. It reminds us of his goodness. In short, thanksgiving forces us to keep God in our thoughts.

We should thank God for all the blessings we can see in our lives—health, friends, guidance, and answered prayer. But we should also verbally thank him for all that is ours that we can't see, such as our adoption as his children, our inheritance in heaven, the ministry of angels in our lives, the new body that will be ours for eternity, and the permanent gift of the Holy Spirit.

By giving thanks, which is simply expressing gratitude for what we have, we prevent our focus from shifting to what we *don't* have. Satan loves to distract God's children from thanksgiving, because he can accomplish much in a heart that is ungrateful. Thanksgiving is a powerful weapon against Satan's tactics.

Supplication. The last step in the ACTS model is supplication—bringing our requests to God. If we are faithful in the first three steps, this last step will not degenerate into a spiritual "shopping list." Too often, when we think of prayer, our minds rush immediately to supplication because we have not cultivated the practice of adoration, confession, and thanksgiving. Supplication by itself can become selfish, but when it follows our adoration, confession, and thanksgiving, it balances our prayer life.

WHAT TO PRAY

Nine times in John's Gospel Jesus commands us to "ask" in prayer. Supplication is God's idea, not just a result of our need. The Lord wants us to ask certain things of him. But what should we pray for? In the Scriptures, God indicates what *he* wishes us to pray for:

Self. Pray for personal growth in Christlikeness and a sensitivity to God (Colossians 1:9–10).

Family. Pray for spouse, children, and children's children; pray for an unbroken heritage of love for God (Proverbs 20:7; Isaiah 54:13).

Community. Pray that God will show us our part in the area where we live (Jeremiah 29:7). Pray for a visible witness of unity among God's people in our communities (Philippians 4:2–3).

Church. Pray for a sense of unity in vision and heart. Pray for a desire to please God rather than each other (Philippians 2:1–4).

Church Leadership. Pray for a deep sensitivity to the will of God, clarity of vision, and a desire for personal holiness (Hebrews 13:17; 1 Timothy 5:17). Pray for a deep conviction for one-on-one disciple making (2 Timothy 2:2).

The Nation. Pray for national repentance and a consciousness of who God is (Psalm 33:12; Proverbs 14:34).

Leaders in Government. Pray for wisdom and integrity, and an awareness of their accountability to God (1 Timothy 2:1–2; Romans 13:1).

Nonbelievers. Pray for understanding of salvation, and an openness to the Spirit's promptings. Pray that Christians will be sensitive to the nonbelievers in their lives (1 Timothy 2:1–6).

The Sick. Pray for God's healing or assurance (James 5:14–16).

Those in Prison. Pray for an understanding of Christ's forgiveness. Pray for strength to resist sin, and encouragement against loneliness (Hebrews 13:3; Colossians 4:18).

Children. Pray for the unborn children who face abortion. Pray for those whose lives are shattered by divorce (Malachi 4:6; Matthew 19:14).

A Weekly Prayer Strategy

MONDAY — Family

- Pray for immediate family members (you may want to get actual requests from them individually).
- Pray for friends of family members.

TUESDAY — Church

- Pray for the leadership in your local fellowship.
- Pray for the marriages and families of your church leadership; they are key targets of Satan.
- Pray for specific ministries within your church.

WEDNESDAY — Community

- Pray for community leaders.
- Pray for the churches in your community.
- Pray for Christian endeavors in your community (e.g., evangelism outreaches, pro-life efforts, ministries to the homeless, etc.).

THURSDAY — Nation

- Pray for our President.
- Pray for elected officials from your state.
- Pray for the seminaries that are training our future pastors and Christian leaders.

FRIDAY — World

- Pray for world peace.
- Pray for the missionaries your church supports.
- Pray for nations that are "closed" to the gospel. (Refer regularly to the "Prayer Concerns Around the World" section at the end of this Journal.)

SATURDAY — Afflicted

- Pray for those ministering in difficult circumstances in developing countries.
- Pray for those in prison.
- Pray for those from your church who are hospitalized or sick.
- Pray for the children affected by divorce.

Ideas

A key element in keeping prayer personal is making it creative. Often, routine is the assassin of effective prayer. Below are some ideas for creative prayer.

- Make a "prayer book" of pictures. This would work well for family, leaders, and missionaries. Often *seeing* people gives us a personal burden as we pray for them.
- When praying for the nation and the world, pray about the front-page events of your local newspaper.
- Make a list of needy people in your church or neighborhood. Pray for them with your family and explore ways that various family members can reach out to them.
- Make a list of all the leaders in your church and their specific areas of ministry. Ask them for specific requests from time to time.
- As you use this Journal and read the suggested Scriptures, keep notes of the needs and people who come to mind and pray for them. Then, think of ways you could help answer each prayer need. For instance, who among your acquaintances needs a "cup of cold water" (Matthew 10:42) from you today?
- Have your family find out more about some of the countries listed in the **"Prayer Concerns"** section (page 129). Using sources such as *National Geographic,* do a pictorial display in a scrap book or on a bulletin board and use that as a focal point for prayer.
- Get a list of all missionaries and organizations your church supports. Many have monthly newsletters that keep you informed so you can pray more specifically. Perhaps pray for one or two missionaries or organizations each month.

We Pray to an Unchanging God

For the Christian, . . . there is deep comfort in the fact that God does not change. . . .

The immutability of God gives us the confidence to pray. This may seem a surprising thing to say. Often people say just the opposite. "If God has already made up his mind, then why should I pray?" The fact that God does not change seems to make prayer unnecessary.

This is a misunderstanding of both God and prayer. We do not pray in order to change God's mind. I suspect that people who think this way have never seriously considered the alternative. Think for a moment how undesirable it would be to pray to a changeable God.

For one thing, even if you could change the mind of Almighty God, would you really want to? You would be asking for your will to be done rather than for his will to be done. But this is the God who made the world and everything in it. He knows everything about you, down to the very hairs of your head. He is the God who in all things "works for the good of those who love him, who have been called according to his purpose" (Rom. 8:28). Do you *really* want to change his mind?

Prayer is not about us getting our way in heaven; it is about God doing his will on earth. As we pray, our desires are conformed to the will of the one "who works out everything in conformity with the purpose of his will" (Eph. 1:11). The only proper way to pray is the way our Lord Jesus taught us to pray: "Your kingdom come, your will be done on earth as it is in heaven" (Matt. 6:10).

—*Philip Graham Ryken*

From Philip Graham Ryken, *Discovering God in Stories from the Bible* (Wheaton, Ill.: Crossway Books, 1999), 78. Used by permission.

Journal Pages

The following pages consist of journal sections for every day of the year. There is a place provided to record your prayer concerns for each day; remember the recommendation that a short, daily prayer time may be better than occasional, longer commitments. There's also a place to record the answers you receive to your prayers. Try to remember what you prayed for from day to day, and be aware of the different ways God may be answering those prayers.

Notice also the suggested daily Scripture readings, which will take you through the entire New Testament in a year. Prayer is conversation with God, and as you read these passages you can think of them as "conversation openers" between you and God. Let him speak to you through his Word, then spend some time with him in prayer. Maybe you'll even find answers to prayer in the suggested daily reading.

Finally, remember the "Prayer Concerns Around the World," listed in the final section of your *Personal Prayer Journal.* The many needs represented can seem overwhelming, yet we must be faithful in prayer, and trust God to meet the needs as he sees fit.

May God bless you as you faithfully seek him in the fellowship of prayer.

PRAYER CONCERNS

5 FRIDAY

—need more love for difficult people
—better balance between job and family
—opportunities to help refugees in town

ANSWERS

Matthew 5:1–26

—learning to "let my light shine" (Matt. 5:16)
—had a whole evening without interruptions!
—will have garage sale to raise money

Come to me, all you who are weary and burdened, and I will give you rest.

—Matthew 11:28

January

JANUARY 2001

S	M	T	W	T	F	S
	1	2	3	4	5	6
7	8	9	10	11	12	13
14	15	16	17	18	19	20
21	22	23	24	25	26	27
28	29	30	31			

PRAYER CONCERNS | **ANSWERS**

31 SUNDAY • DECEMBER

1 MONDAY — Matthew 1

2 TUESDAY — Matthew 2

Thou hast made us for Thyself, O Lord, and our hearts are restless until they rest in Thee.

—St. Augustine

PRAYER CONCERNS | **ANSWERS**

3 WEDNESDAY — Matthew 3

4 THURSDAY — Matthew 4

5 FRIDAY — Matthew 5:1–26

6 SATURDAY — Matthew 5:27–48

January

Pray in the Spirit on all occasions with all kinds of prayers and requests.
—Ephesians 6:18

JANUARY 2001

S	M	T	W	T	F	S
	1	2	3	4	5	6
7	8	9	10	11	12	13
14	15	16	17	18	19	20
21	22	23	24	25	26	27
28	29	30	31			

PRAYER CONCERNS	ANSWERS
7 SUNDAY	Matthew 6:1–18
8 MONDAY	Matthew 6:19–34
9 TUESDAY	Matthew 7

Is prayer your steering wheel or your spare tire?

—*Corrie ten Boom*

PRAYER CONCERNS	**ANSWERS**
10 WEDNESDAY	Matthew 8:1–17
11 THURSDAY	Matthew 8:18–34
12 FRIDAY	Matthew 9:1–17
13 SATURDAY	Matthew 9:18–38

Those who hope in the LORD will renew their strength.

—Isaiah 40:31

January

JANUARY 2001

S	M	T	W	T	F	S
	1	2	3	4	5	6
7	8	9	10	11	12	13
14	15	16	17	18	19	20
21	22	23	24	25	26	27
28	29	30	31			

PRAYER CONCERNS | **ANSWERS**

14 SUNDAY — Matthew 10:1–20

15 MONDAY — Matthew 10:21–42

16 TUESDAY — Matthew 11

God never imposes a duty without giving time to do it.

—*John Ruskin*

PRAYER CONCERNS	ANSWERS
17 WEDNESDAY	Matthew 12:1–23
18 THURSDAY	Matthew 12:24–50
19 FRIDAY	Matthew 13:1–30
20 SATURDAY	Matthew 13:31–58

Set an example for the believers in speech, in life, in love, in faith and in purity.

—1 Timothy 4:12

January

JANUARY 2001

S	M	T	W	T	F	S
	1	2	3	4	5	6
7	8	9	10	11	12	13
14	15	16	17	18	19	20
21	22	23	24	25	26	27
28	29	30	31			

PRAYER CONCERNS	ANSWERS
21 SUNDAY	Matthew 14:1–21
22 MONDAY	Matthew 14:22–36
23 TUESDAY	Matthew 15:1–20

A good example is the best sermon.

—Benjamin Franklin

PRAYER CONCERNS	ANSWERS
24 WEDNESDAY	Matthew 15:21–39
25 THURSDAY	Matthew 16
26 FRIDAY	Matthew 17
27 SATURDAY	Matthew 18:1–20

January

Righteousness exalts a nation, but sin is a disgrace to any people.
—Proverbs 14:34

JANUARY 2001						
S	M	T	W	T	F	S
	1	2	3	4	5	6
7	8	9	10	11	12	13
14	15	16	17	18	19	20
21	22	23	24	25	26	27
28	29	30	31			

PRAYER CONCERNS	ANSWERS
28 SUNDAY	Matthew 18:21–35
29 MONDAY	Matthew 19
30 TUESDAY	Matthew 20:1–16

If we are not governed by God, then we will be ruled by tyrants.

—*William Penn*

PRAYER CONCERNS | **ANSWERS**

31 WEDNESDAY — Matthew 20:17–34

1 THURSDAY • FEBRUARY — Matthew 21:1–22

2 FRIDAY — Matthew 21:23–46

3 SATURDAY — Matthew 22:1–22

Each of you should look not only to your own interests, but also to the interests of others.

—Philippians 2:4

February

FEBRUARY 2001

S	M	T	W	T	F	S
				1	2	3
4	5	6	7	8	9	10
11	12	13	14	15	16	17
18	19	20	21	22	23	24
25	26	27	28			

PRAYER CONCERNS | **ANSWERS**

4 SUNDAY — Matthew 22:23–46

5 MONDAY — Matthew 23:1–22

6 TUESDAY — Matthew 23:23–39

There is no prayer so blessed as the prayer which asks for nothing.

—O. J. Simon

PRAYER CONCERNS | **ANSWERS**

7 WEDNESDAY

Matthew 24:1–28

8 THURSDAY

Matthew 24:29–51

9 FRIDAY

Matthew 25:1–30

10 SATURDAY

Matthew 25:31–46

February

May the Lord make your love increase and overflow for each other.
—1 Thessalonians 3:12

FEBRUARY 2001						
S	M	T	W	T	F	S
				1	2	3
4	5	6	7	8	9	10
11	12	13	14	15	16	17
18	19	20	21	22	23	24
25	26	27	28			

PRAYER CONCERNS | **ANSWERS**

11 SUNDAY — Matthew 26:1–25

12 MONDAY — Matthew 26:26–50

13 TUESDAY — Matthew 26:51–75

He who sees a need and waits to be asked for help is as unkind as if he had refused it.

—*Dante*

PRAYER CONCERNS	ANSWERS
14 WEDNESDAY	Matthew 27:1–26
15 THURSDAY	Matthew 27:27–50
16 FRIDAY	Matthew 27:51–66
17 SATURDAY	Matthew 28

February

Let the word of Christ dwell in you richly.
—Colossians 3:16

FEBRUARY 2001						
S	M	T	W	T	F	S
				1	2	3
4	5	6	7	8	9	10
11	12	13	14	15	16	17
18	19	20	21	22	23	24
25	26	27	28			

PRAYER CONCERNS | **ANSWERS**

18 SUNDAY — Mark 1:1–22

19 MONDAY — Mark 1:23–45

20 TUESDAY — Mark 2

Lack of wealth is easily repaired; but poverty of soul is irreparable.

—Michel de Montaigne

PRAYER CONCERNS | **ANSWERS**

21 WEDNESDAY — Mark 3:1–19

22 THURSDAY — Mark 3:20–35

23 FRIDAY — Mark 4:1–20

24 SATURDAY — Mark 4:21–41

Do not be anxious about anything, but in everything, by prayer and petition, with thanksgiving, present your requests to God.

—Philippians 4:6

February

FEBRUARY 2001						
S	M	T	W	T	F	S
				1	2	3
4	5	6	7	8	9	10
11	12	13	14	15	16	17
18	19	20	21	22	23	24
25	26	27	28			

PRAYER CONCERNS	ANSWERS
25 SUNDAY	Mark 5:1–20
26 MONDAY	Mark 5:21–43
27 TUESDAY	Mark 6:1–29

Anxiety is the natural result when our hopes are centered in anything short of God and his will for us.

—*Billy Graham*

PRAYER CONCERNS	ANSWERS
28 WEDNESDAY	Mark 6:30–56
1 THURSDAY • MARCH	Mark 7
2 FRIDAY	Mark 8:1–21
3 SATURDAY	Mark 8:22–38

March

He who began a good work in you will carry it on to completion until the day of Christ Jesus.
—Philippians 1:6

MARCH 2001						
S	M	T	W	T	F	S
				1	2	3
4	5	6	7	8	9	10
11	12	13	14	15	16	17
18	19	20	21	22	23	24
25	26	27	28	29	30	31

PRAYER CONCERNS	ANSWERS
4 SUNDAY	Mark 9:1–29
5 MONDAY	Mark 9:30–50
6 TUESDAY	Mark 10:1–31

Fear not that thy life shall come to an end, but rather fear that it shall never have a beginning.

—John Henry Newman

PRAYER CONCERNS	ANSWERS
7 WEDNESDAY	Mark 10:32–52
8 THURSDAY	Mark 11:1–18
9 FRIDAY	Mark 11:19–33
10 SATURDAY	Mark 12:1–27

March

Man is destined to die once, and after that to face judgment.

—Hebrews 9:27

MARCH 2001

S	M	T	W	T	F	S
				1	2	3
4	5	6	7	8	9	10
11	12	13	14	15	16	17
18	19	20	21	22	23	24
25	26	27	28	29	30	31

PRAYER CONCERNS **ANSWERS**

11 SUNDAY — Mark 12:28–44

12 MONDAY — Mark 13:1–20

13 TUESDAY — Mark 13:21–37

God hath given to man a short time here upon earth, and yet upon this short time eternity depends.

—*Jeremy Taylor*

PRAYER CONCERNS | **ANSWERS**

14 WEDNESDAY — Mark 14:1–26

15 THURSDAY — Mark 14:27–53

16 FRIDAY — Mark 14:54–72

17 SATURDAY — Mark 15:1–25

March

Live a life of love, just as Christ loved us and gave himself up for us.

—Ephesians 5:2

MARCH 2001						
S	M	T	W	T	F	S
				1	2	3
4	5	6	7	8	9	10
11	12	13	14	15	16	17
18	19	20	21	22	23	24
25	26	27	28	29	30	31

PRAYER CONCERNS | **ANSWERS**

18 SUNDAY — Mark 15:26–47

19 MONDAY — Mark 16

20 TUESDAY — Luke 1:1–20

It is only the souls that do not love that go empty in this world.

—*Robert Hugh Benson*

PRAYER CONCERNS	ANSWERS
21 WEDNESDAY	Luke 1:21–38
22 THURSDAY	Luke 1:39–56
23 FRIDAY	Luke 1:57–80
24 SATURDAY	Luke 2:1–24

March

God opposes the proud but gives grace to the humble.

—1 Peter 5:5

MARCH 2001						
S	M	T	W	T	F	S
				1	2	3
4	5	6	7	8	9	10
11	12	13	14	15	16	17
18	19	20	21	22	23	24
25	26	27	28	29	30	31

PRAYER CONCERNS	ANSWERS
25 SUNDAY	Luke 2:25–52
26 MONDAY	Luke 3
27 TUESDAY	Luke 4:1–30

No really great man ever thought himself so.

—*William Hazlitt*

PRAYER CONCERNS | **ANSWERS**

28 WEDNESDAY — Luke 4:31–44

29 THURSDAY — Luke 5:1–16

30 FRIDAY — Luke 5:17–39

31 SATURDAY — Luke 6:1–26

For God so loved the world that he gave his one and only Son, that whoever believes in him shall not perish but have eternal life.

—John 3:16

April

APRIL 2001

S	M	T	W	T	F	S
1	2	3	4	5	6	7
8	9	10	11	12	13	14
15	16	17	18	19	20	21
22	23	24	25	26	27	28
29	30					

PRAYER CONCERNS	ANSWERS
1 SUNDAY	Luke 6:27–49
2 MONDAY	Luke 7:1–30
3 TUESDAY	Luke 7:31–50

The divine love hovers over the life of man with the vivacious persistence of April calling earth to life.

—*Walter Farrell*

PRAYER CONCERNS	**ANSWERS**
4 WEDNESDAY	Luke 8:1–25
5 THURSDAY	Luke 8:26–56
6 FRIDAY	Luke 9:1–17
7 SATURDAY	Luke 9:18–36

Be very careful, then, how you live—not as unwise but as wise, making the most of every opportunity.

—Ephesians 5:15–16

April

APRIL 2001

S	M	T	W	T	F	S
1	2	3	4	5	6	7
8	9	10	11	12	13	14
15	16	17	18	19	20	21
22	23	24	25	26	27	28
29	30					

PRAYER CONCERNS | **ANSWERS**

8 SUNDAY — Luke 9:37–62

9 MONDAY — Luke 10:1–24

10 TUESDAY — Luke 10:25–42

Millions long for immortality who do not know what to do with themselves on a rainy Sunday afternoon.

—Susan Ertz

PRAYER CONCERNS | **ANSWERS**

11 WEDNESDAY — Luke 11:1–28

12 THURSDAY — Luke 11:29–54

13 FRIDAY — Luke 12:1–31

14 SATURDAY — Luke 12:32–59

Because he himself suffered when he was tempted, he is able to help those who are being tempted.

—Hebrews 2:18

April

APRIL 2001

S	M	T	W	T	F	S
1	2	3	4	5	6	7
8	9	10	11	12	13	14
15	16	17	18	19	20	21
22	23	24	25	26	27	28
29	30					

PRAYER CONCERNS	ANSWERS
15 SUNDAY	Luke 13:1–22
16 MONDAY	Luke 13:23–35
17 TUESDAY	Luke 14:1–24

I have more trouble with D. L. Moody than with any other man I ever met.

—D. L. Moody

PRAYER CONCERNS	ANSWERS
18 WEDNESDAY	Luke 14:25–35
19 THURSDAY	Luke 15:1–10
20 FRIDAY	Luke 15:11–32
21 SATURDAY	Luke 16

I will praise you, O LORD, with all my heart; I will tell of all your wonders. I will be glad and rejoice in you; I will sing praise to your name, O Most High.

—Psalm 9:1–2

April

APRIL 2001

S	M	T	W	T	F	S
1	2	3	4	5	6	7
8	9	10	11	12	13	14
15	16	17	18	19	20	21
22	23	24	25	26	27	28
29	30					

PRAYER CONCERNS | **ANSWERS**

22 SUNDAY — Luke 17:1–19

23 MONDAY — Luke 17:20–37

24 TUESDAY — Luke 18:1–23

When God measures man, He puts the tape around his heart—not his head.

—*Guideposts*

PRAYER CONCERNS	ANSWERS
25 WEDNESDAY	Luke 18:24–43
26 THURSDAY	Luke 19:1–27
27 FRIDAY	Luke 19:28–48
28 SATURDAY	Luke 20:1–26

It is more blessed to give than to receive.

—Acts 20:35

MAY 2001						
S	M	T	W	T	F	S
		1	2	3	4	5
6	7	8	9	10	11	12
13	14	15	16	17	18	19
20	21	22	23	24	25	26
27	28	29	30	31		

PRAYER CONCERNS	ANSWERS
29 SUNDAY • APRIL	Luke 20:27–47
30 MONDAY	Luke 21:1–19
1 TUESDAY	Luke 21:20–38

Generosity gives help rather than advice.

—*Luc de Clapiers Vauvenargues*

PRAYER CONCERNS	**ANSWERS**
2 WEDNESDAY	Luke 22:1–20
3 THURSDAY	Luke 22:21–46
4 FRIDAY	Luke 22:47–71
5 SATURDAY	Luke 23:1–25

May

Cast but a glance at riches, and they are gone, for they will surely sprout wings and fly off to the sky like an eagle.

—Proverbs 23:5

MAY 2001

S	M	T	W	T	F	S
		1	2	3	4	5
6	7	8	9	10	11	12
13	14	15	16	17	18	19
20	21	22	23	24	25	26
27	28	29	30	31		

PRAYER CONCERNS | **ANSWERS**

6 SUNDAY | Luke 23:26–56

7 MONDAY | Luke 24:1–35

8 TUESDAY | Luke 24:36–53

Make happiness the object of your pursuit, and it leads you on a wild-goose chase.

—*Nathaniel Hawthorne*

PRAYER CONCERNS	ANSWERS
9 WEDNESDAY	John 1:1–28
10 THURSDAY	John 1:29–51
11 FRIDAY	John 2
12 SATURDAY	John 3:1–18

A generous man will prosper; he who refreshes others will himself be refreshed.

—Proverbs 11:25

MAY 2001						
S	M	T	W	T	F	S
		1	2	3	4	5
6	7	8	9	10	11	12
13	14	15	16	17	18	19
20	21	22	23	24	25	26
27	28	29	30	31		

PRAYER CONCERNS	ANSWERS
13 SUNDAY	John 3:19–36
14 MONDAY	John 4:1–30
15 TUESDAY	John 4:31–54

When a man is all wrapped up in himself he makes a pretty small package.

—*John Ruskin*

PRAYER CONCERNS	ANSWERS
16 WEDNESDAY	John 5:1–24
17 THURSDAY	John 5:25–47
18 FRIDAY	John 6:1–21
19 SATURDAY	John 6:22–44

May

No one can serve two masters. . . . You cannot serve both God and Money.

—Matthew 6:24

MAY 2001

S	M	T	W	T	F	S
		1	2	3	4	5
6	7	8	9	10	11	12
13	14	15	16	17	18	19
20	21	22	23	24	25	26
27	28	29	30	31		

PRAYER CONCERNS	ANSWERS
20 SUNDAY	John 6:45–71
21 MONDAY	John 7:1–27
22 TUESDAY	John 7:28–53

Money is a good servant but a bad master.

—*Proverb*

PRAYER CONCERNS

23 WEDNESDAY

ANSWERS

John 8:1–27

24 THURSDAY

John 8:28–59

25 FRIDAY

John 9:1–23

26 SATURDAY

John 9:24–41

If a man shuts his ears to the cry of the poor, he too will cry out and not be answered.

—Proverbs 21:13

MAY 2001						
S	M	T	W	T	F	S
		1	2	3	4	5
6	7	8	9	10	11	12
13	14	15	16	17	18	19
20	21	22	23	24	25	26
27	28	29	30	31		

PRAYER CONCERNS	ANSWERS
27 SUNDAY	John 10:1–23
28 MONDAY	John 10:24–42
29 TUESDAY	John 11:1–29

Let my heart be broken with the things that break the heart of God.

—*Robert Pierce*

PRAYER CONCERNS | **ANSWERS**

30 WEDNESDAY — John 11:30–57

31 THURSDAY — John 12:1–26

1 FRIDAY • JUNE — John 12:27–50

2 SATURDAY — John 13:1–20

Whoever can be trusted with very little can also be trusted with much, and whoever is dishonest with very little will also be dishonest with much.

—Luke 16:10

June

JUNE 2001

S	M	T	W	T	F	S
					1	2
3	4	5	6	7	8	9
10	11	12	13	14	15	16
17	18	19	20	21	22	23
24	25	26	27	28	29	30

PRAYER CONCERNS | **ANSWERS**

3 SUNDAY — John 13:21–38

4 MONDAY — John 14

5 TUESDAY — John 15

If a man cannot be a Christian in the place where he is, he cannot be a Christian anywhere.

—Henry Ward Beecher

PRAYER CONCERNS	ANSWERS
6 WEDNESDAY	John 16
7 THURSDAY	John 17
8 FRIDAY	John 18:1–18
9 SATURDAY	John 18:19–40

June

Let us fix our eyes on Jesus, the author and perfecter of our faith.

—Hebrews 12:2

JUNE 2001						
S	M	T	W	T	F	S
					1	2
3	4	5	6	7	8	9
10	11	12	13	14	15	16
17	18	19	20	21	22	23
24	25	26	27	28	29	30

PRAYER CONCERNS	ANSWERS
10 SUNDAY	John 19:1–22
11 MONDAY	John 19:23–42
12 TUESDAY	John 20

A man who wants to lead the orchestra must turn his back on the crowd.

—Max Lucado

PRAYER CONCERNS	**ANSWERS**
13 WEDNESDAY	John 21
14 THURSDAY	Acts 1
15 FRIDAY	Acts 2:1–21
16 SATURDAY	Acts 2:22–47

June

Love . . . is not
self-seeking.
—1 Corinthians 13:4–5

JUNE 2001

S	M	T	W	T	F	S
					1	2
3	4	5	6	7	8	9
10	11	12	13	14	15	16
17	18	19	20	21	22	23
24	25	26	27	28	29	30

PRAYER CONCERNS | **ANSWERS**

17 SUNDAY — Acts 3

18 MONDAY — Acts 4:1–22

19 TUESDAY — Acts 4:23–37

The only reward love seeks is someone to love. If you are looking for something else, it isn't love.

—*Bernard of Clairvaux*

PRAYER CONCERNS	ANSWERS
20 WEDNESDAY	Acts 5:1–21
21 THURSDAY	Acts 5:22–42
22 FRIDAY	Acts 6
23 SATURDAY	Acts 7:1–21

As long as it is day, we must do the work of him who sent me. Night is coming, when no one can work.

—John 9:4

June

JUNE 2001

S	M	T	W	T	F	S
					1	2
3	4	5	6	7	8	9
10	11	12	13	14	15	16
17	18	19	20	21	22	23
24	25	26	27	28	29	30

PRAYER CONCERNS	ANSWERS
24 SUNDAY	Acts 7:22–43
25 MONDAY	Acts 7:44–60
26 TUESDAY	Acts 8:1–25

If the Devil finds a man idle, he'll set him to work.

—*James Kelly*

PRAYER CONCERNS | **ANSWERS**

27 WEDNESDAY — Acts 8:26–40

28 THURSDAY — Acts 9:1–21

29 FRIDAY — Acts 9:22–43

30 SATURDAY — Acts 10:1–23

July

Whom have I in heaven but you? And being with you, I desire nothing on earth.

—Psalm 73:25

JULY 2001						
S	M	T	W	T	F	S
1	2	3	4	5	6	7
8	9	10	11	12	13	14
15	16	17	18	19	20	21
22	23	24	25	26	27	28
29	30	31				

PRAYER CONCERNS	ANSWERS
1 SUNDAY	Acts 10:24–48
2 MONDAY	Acts 11
3 TUESDAY	Acts 12

You shall have joy, or you shall have power, said God; you shall not have both.

—*Ralph Waldo Emerson*

PRAYER CONCERNS	ANSWERS
4 WEDNESDAY	Acts 13:1–25
5 THURSDAY	Acts 13:26–52
6 FRIDAY	Acts 14
7 SATURDAY	Acts 15:1–21

Let us not become weary in doing good, for at the proper time we will reap a harvest if we do not give up.

—Galatians 6:9

July

JULY 2001

S	M	T	W	T	F	S
1	2	3	4	5	6	7
8	9	10	11	12	13	14
15	16	17	18	19	20	21
22	23	24	25	26	27	28
29	30	31				

PRAYER CONCERNS | **ANSWERS**

8 SUNDAY

Acts 15:22–41

9 MONDAY

Acts 16:1–21

10 TUESDAY

Acts 16:22–40

He who labors as he prays lifts his heart to God with his hands.

—*Bernard of Clairvaux*

PRAYER CONCERNS | **ANSWERS**

11 WEDNESDAY

Acts 17:1–15

12 THURSDAY

Acts 17:16–34

13 FRIDAY

Acts 18

14 SATURDAY

Acts 19:1–20

July

There is no fear in love. But perfect love drives out fear.

—1 John 4:18

JULY 2001						
S	M	T	W	T	F	S
1	2	3	4	5	6	7
8	9	10	11	12	13	14
15	16	17	18	19	20	21
22	23	24	25	26	27	28
29	30	31				

PRAYER CONCERNS | **ANSWERS**

15 SUNDAY — Acts 19:21–41

16 MONDAY — Acts 20:1–16

17 TUESDAY — Acts 20:17–38

Live in such a way as not to be afraid to die.

—*Teresa of Avila*

PRAYER CONCERNS

ANSWERS

18 WEDNESDAY

Acts 21:1–17

19 THURSDAY

Acts 21:18–40

20 FRIDAY

Acts 22

21 SATURDAY

Acts 23:1–15

Seek first his kingdom
and his righteousness,
and all these things will
be given to you as well.
—Matthew 6:33

July

JULY 2001

S	M	T	W	T	F	S
1	2	3	4	5	6	7
8	9	10	11	12	13	14
15	16	17	18	19	20	21
22	23	24	25	26	27	28
29	30	31				

PRAYER CONCERNS	ANSWERS
22 SUNDAY	Acts 23:16–35
23 MONDAY	Acts 24
24 TUESDAY	Acts 25

The great use of a life is to spend it for something that outlasts it.
—*William James*

PRAYER CONCERNS | **ANSWERS**

25 WEDNESDAY — Acts 26

26 THURSDAY — Acts 27:1–26

27 FRIDAY — Acts 27:27–44

28 SATURDAY — Acts 28

The LORD is close to the brokenhearted and saves those who are crushed in spirit.

—Psalm 34:18

July

JULY 2001						
S	M	T	W	T	F	S
1	2	3	4	5	6	7
8	9	10	11	12	13	14
15	16	17	18	19	20	21
22	23	24	25	26	27	28
29	30	31				

PRAYER CONCERNS	ANSWERS
29 SUNDAY	Romans 1
30 MONDAY	Romans 2
31 TUESDAY	Romans 3

Earth has no sorrow that Heaven cannot heal.

—*Thomas More*

PRAYER CONCERNS	ANSWERS
1 WEDNESDAY • AUGUST	Romans 4
2 THURSDAY	Romans 5
3 FRIDAY	Romans 6
4 SATURDAY	Romans 7

In the same way, let your light shine before men, that they may see your good deeds and praise your Father in heaven.

—Matthew 5:16

August

AUGUST 2001

S	M	T	W	T	F	S
			1	2	3	4
5	6	7	8	9	10	11
12	13	14	15	16	17	18
19	20	21	22	23	24	25
26	27	28	29	30	31	

PRAYER CONCERNS	ANSWERS
5 SUNDAY	Romans 8:1–21
6 MONDAY	Romans 8:22–39
7 TUESDAY	Romans 9:1–15

Let us so live that when we come to die even the undertaker will be sorry.

—*Mark Twain*

PRAYER CONCERNS | **ANSWERS**

8 WEDNESDAY — Romans 9:16–33

9 THURSDAY — Romans 10

10 FRIDAY — Romans 11:1–18

11 SATURDAY — Romans 11:19–36

Those who hope in the LORD will renew their strength. They will soar on wings like eagles; they will run and not grow weary, they will walk and not be faint.

—Isaiah 40:31

August

AUGUST 2001						
S	M	T	W	T	F	S
			1	2	3	4
5	6	7	8	9	10	11
12	13	14	15	16	17	18
19	20	21	22	23	24	25
26	27	28	29	30	31	

PRAYER CONCERNS	ANSWERS
12 SUNDAY	Romans 12
13 MONDAY	Romans 13
14 TUESDAY	Romans 14

Do not wait for great strength before setting out, for immobility will weaken you further.

—*Philippe Vernier*

PRAYER CONCERNS	ANSWERS
15 WEDNESDAY	Romans 15:1–13
16 THURSDAY	Romans 15:14–33
17 FRIDAY	Romans 16
18 SATURDAY	1 Corinthians 1

Dear friends, let us love one another, for love comes from God. Everyone who loves has been born of God and knows God.

—1 John 4:7

August

AUGUST 2001

S	M	T	W	T	F	S
			1	2	3	4
5	6	7	8	9	10	11
12	13	14	15	16	17	18
19	20	21	22	23	24	25
26	27	28	29	30	31	

PRAYER CONCERNS | **ANSWERS**

19 SUNDAY — 1 Corinthians 2

20 MONDAY — 1 Corinthians 3

21 TUESDAY — 1 Corinthians 4

No man is useless while he has a friend.

—*Robert Louis Stevenson*

PRAYER CONCERNS	ANSWERS
22 WEDNESDAY	1 Corinthians 5
23 THURSDAY	1 Corinthians 6
24 FRIDAY	1 Corinthians 7:1–19
25 SATURDAY	1 Corinthians 7:20–40

Let us be thankful, and so worship God acceptably with reverence and awe, for our "God is a consuming fire."

—Hebrews 12:28–29

August

AUGUST 2001

S	M	T	W	T	F	S
			1	2	3	4
5	6	7	8	9	10	11
12	13	14	15	16	17	18
19	20	21	22	23	24	25
26	27	28	29	30	31	

PRAYER CONCERNS | **ANSWERS**

26 SUNDAY

1 Corinthians 8

27 MONDAY

1 Corinthians 9

28 TUESDAY

1 Corinthians 10:1–18

To serve God with fear is good; to serve Him out of love is better; but to fear and love Him together is best of all.

—Meister Eckehart

PRAYER CONCERNS | **ANSWERS**

29 WEDNESDAY

1 Corinthians 10:19–33

30 THURSDAY

1 Corinthians 11:1–16

31 FRIDAY

1 Corinthians 11:17–34

1 SATURDAY • SEPTEMBER

1 Corinthians 12

Here is the conclusion of the matter: Fear God and keep his commandments, for this is the whole duty of man.

—Ecclesiastes 12:13

September

SEPTEMBER 2001

S	M	T	W	T	F	S
						1
2	3	4	5	6	7	8
9	10	11	12	13	14	15
16	17	18	19	20	21	22
23/30	24	25	26	27	28	29

PRAYER CONCERNS | **ANSWERS**

2 SUNDAY

1 Corinthians 13

3 MONDAY

1 Corinthians 14:1–20

4 TUESDAY

1 Corinthians 14:21–40

As soon as I believed there was a God, I understood I could not do otherwise than live for Him alone.

—Charles de Foucauld

PRAYER CONCERNS	**ANSWERS**
5 WEDNESDAY	1 Corinthians 15:1–28
6 THURSDAY	1 Corinthians 15:29–58
7 FRIDAY	1 Corinthians 16
8 SATURDAY	2 Corinthians 1

I am the way and the truth and the life. No one comes to the Father except through me.

—John 14:6

September

SEPTEMBER 2001

S	M	T	W	T	F	S
						1
2	3	4	5	6	7	8
9	10	11	12	13	14	15
16	17	18	19	20	21	22
23/30	24	25	26	27	28	29

PRAYER CONCERNS | **ANSWERS**

9 SUNDAY — 2 Corinthians 2

10 MONDAY — 2 Corinthians 3

11 TUESDAY — 2 Corinthians 4

To come to God there is a straight line for every man everywhere.
—*John Donne*

PRAYER CONCERNS | **ANSWERS**

12 WEDNESDAY — 2 Corinthians 5

13 THURSDAY — 2 Corinthians 6

14 FRIDAY — 2 Corinthians 7

15 SATURDAY — 2 Corinthians 8

September

Seek the LORD while he may be found; call on him while he is near.
—Isaiah 55:6

SEPTEMBER 2001						
S	M	T	W	T	F	S
						1
2	3	4	5	6	7	8
9	10	11	12	13	14	15
16	17	18	19	20	21	22
23/30	24	25	26	27	28	29

PRAYER CONCERNS | **ANSWERS**

16 SUNDAY

2 Corinthians 9

17 MONDAY

2 Corinthians 10

18 TUESDAY

2 Corinthians 11:1–15

Ever since the days of Adam, man has been hiding from God and saying, "God is hard to find."

—Fulton J. Sheen

PRAYER CONCERNS | **ANSWERS**

19 WEDNESDAY

2 Corinthians 11:16–33

20 THURSDAY

2 Corinthians 12

21 FRIDAY

2 Corinthians 13

22 SATURDAY

Galatians 1

Be kind and compassionate to one another, forgiving each other, just as in Christ God forgave you.

—Ephesians 4:32

September

SEPTEMBER 2001

S	M	T	W	T	F	S
						1
2	3	4	5	6	7	8
9	10	11	12	13	14	15
16	17	18	19	20	21	22
23/30	24	25	26	27	28	29

PRAYER CONCERNS | **ANSWERS**

23 SUNDAY — Galatians 2

24 MONDAY — Galatians 3

25 TUESDAY — Galatians 4

Mercy imitates God, and disappoints Satan.

—John Chrysostom

PRAYER CONCERNS | **ANSWERS**

26 WEDNESDAY | Galatians 5

27 THURSDAY | Galatians 6

28 FRIDAY | Ephesians 1

29 SATURDAY | Ephesians 2

October

Godliness with content-
ment is great gain. For
we brought nothing into
the world, and we can
take nothing out of it.
—1 Timothy 6:6–7

OCTOBER 2001						
S	M	T	W	T	F	S
	1	2	3	4	5	6
7	8	9	10	11	12	13
14	15	16	17	18	19	20
21	22	23	24	25	26	27
28	29	30	31			

PRAYER CONCERNS	ANSWERS
30 SUNDAY • SEPTEMBER	Ephesians 3
1 MONDAY	Ephesians 4
2 TUESDAY	Ephesians 5:1–16

Shrouds have no pockets.

—*Proverb*

PRAYER CONCERNS	ANSWERS
3 WEDNESDAY	Ephesians 5:17–33
4 THURSDAY	Ephesians 6
5 FRIDAY	Philippians 1
6 SATURDAY	Philippians 2

October

Anyone, then, who knows the good he ought to do and doesn't do it, sins.

—James 4:17

OCTOBER 2001						
S	M	T	W	T	F	S
	1	2	3	4	5	6
7	8	9	10	11	12	13
14	15	16	17	18	19	20
21	22	23	24	25	26	27
28	29	30	31			

PRAYER CONCERNS	ANSWERS
7 SUNDAY	Philippians 3
8 MONDAY	Philippians 4
9 TUESDAY	Colossians 1

The time will come when thou wilt wish for one day or hour to amend, and I know not whither thou shalt obtain it.

—*Thomas à Kempis*

PRAYER CONCERNS	ANSWERS
10 WEDNESDAY	Colossians 2
11 THURSDAY	Colossians 3
12 FRIDAY	Colossians 4
13 SATURDAY	1 Thessalonians 1

If we confess our sins, he is faithful and just and will forgive us our sins and purify us from all unrighteousness.

—1 John 1:9

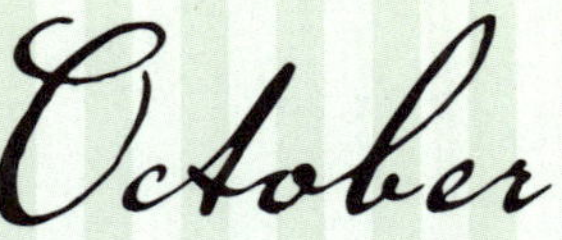

OCTOBER 2001

S	M	T	W	T	F	S
	1	2	3	4	5	6
7	8	9	10	11	12	13
14	15	16	17	18	19	20
21	22	23	24	25	26	27
28	29	30	31			

PRAYER CONCERNS	ANSWERS
14 SUNDAY	1 Thessalonians 2
15 MONDAY	1 Thessalonians 3
16 TUESDAY	1 Thessalonians 4

Perfection is achieved not by never falling, but by rising every time we fall.

—*John A. O'Brien*

PRAYER CONCERNS	ANSWERS
17 WEDNESDAY	1 Thessalonians 5
18 THURSDAY	2 Thessalonians 1
19 FRIDAY	2 Thessalonians 2
20 SATURDAY	2 Thessalonians 3

Clothe yourselves with the Lord Jesus Christ, and do not think about how to gratify the desires of the sinful nature.

—Romans 13:14

October

OCTOBER 2001

S	M	T	W	T	F	S
	1	2	3	4	5	6
7	8	9	10	11	12	13
14	15	16	17	18	19	20
21	22	23	24	25	26	27
28	29	30	31			

PRAYER CONCERNS	ANSWERS
21 SUNDAY	1 Timothy 1
22 MONDAY	1 Timothy 2
23 TUESDAY	1 Timothy 3

That thou mayest have pleasure in everything, seek pleasure in nothing.

—St. John of the Cross

PRAYER CONCERNS	**ANSWERS**
24 WEDNESDAY	1 Timothy 4
25 THURSDAY	1 Timothy 5
26 FRIDAY	1 Timothy 6
27 SATURDAY	2 Timothy 1

Whatever was to my profit I now consider loss for the sake of Christ. . . . I consider everything a loss compared to the surpassing greatness of knowing Christ Jesus my Lord.

—Philippians 3:7–8

October

OCTOBER 2001

S	M	T	W	T	F	S
	1	2	3	4	5	6
7	8	9	10	11	12	13
14	15	16	17	18	19	20
21	22	23	24	25	26	27
28	29	30	31			

PRAYER CONCERNS	ANSWERS
28 SUNDAY	2 Timothy 2
29 MONDAY	2 Timothy 3
30 TUESDAY	2 Timothy 4

Each stage of a progressive prayer-life is a stage in the putting to death of the self that God may work and reign.

—*E. Herman*

PRAYER CONCERNS | **ANSWERS**

31 WEDNESDAY — Titus 1

1 THURSDAY • NOVEMBER — Titus 2

2 FRIDAY — Titus 3

3 SATURDAY — Philemon

November

Love one another deeply, from the heart.

—1 Peter 1:22

NOVEMBER 2001						
S	M	T	W	T	F	S
				1	2	3
4	5	6	7	8	9	10
11	12	13	14	15	16	17
18	19	20	21	22	23	24
25	26	27	28	29	30	

PRAYER CONCERNS	ANSWERS
4 SUNDAY	Hebrews 1
5 MONDAY	Hebrews 2
6 TUESDAY	Hebrews 3

The most prevalent failure of Christian love is the failure to express it.

—Paul E. Johnson

PRAYER CONCERNS	ANSWERS
7 WEDNESDAY	Hebrews 4
8 THURSDAY	Hebrews 5
9 FRIDAY	Hebrews 6
10 SATURDAY	Hebrews 7

All men are like grass,
and all their glory is like
the flowers of the field;
the grass withers and
the flowers fall, but the
word of the Lord stands
forever.

—1 Peter 1:24–25

November

NOVEMBER 2001

S	M	T	W	T	F	S
				1	2	3
4	5	6	7	8	9	10
11	12	13	14	15	16	17
18	19	20	21	22	23	24
25	26	27	28	29	30	

PRAYER CONCERNS | **ANSWERS**

11 SUNDAY — Hebrews 8

12 MONDAY — Hebrews 9

13 TUESDAY — Hebrews 10:1–18

The more moral a man is the more desperately he needs . . . prayer, [to] humble him in his own eyes.

—J. V. L. Casserley

PRAYER CONCERNS	ANSWERS
14 WEDNESDAY	Hebrews 10:19–39
15 THURSDAY	Hebrews 11:1–19
16 FRIDAY	Hebrews 11:20–40
17 SATURDAY	Hebrews 12

We do not know what we ought to pray for, but the Spirit himself intercedes for us with groans that words cannot express.

—Romans 8:26

November

NOVEMBER 2001

S	M	T	W	T	F	S
				1	2	3
4	5	6	7	8	9	10
11	12	13	14	15	16	17
18	19	20	21	22	23	24
25	26	27	28	29	30	

PRAYER CONCERNS | **ANSWERS**

18 SUNDAY — Hebrews 13

19 MONDAY — James 1

20 TUESDAY — James 2

In most cases prayer consists more in groaning than in speaking, in tears rather than in words.

—St. Augustine

PRAYER CONCERNS	ANSWERS
21 WEDNESDAY	James 3
22 THURSDAY	James 4
23 FRIDAY	James 5
24 SATURDAY	1 Peter 1

"Even now," declares the LORD, "return to me with all your heart, with fasting and weeping and mourning."

—Joel 2:12

November

NOVEMBER 2001

S	M	T	W	T	F	S
				1	2	3
4	5	6	7	8	9	10
11	12	13	14	15	16	17
18	19	20	21	22	23	24
25	26	27	28	29	30	

PRAYER CONCERNS	ANSWERS
25 SUNDAY	1 Peter 2
26 MONDAY	1 Peter 3
27 TUESDAY	1 Peter 4

There is in repentance this beautiful mystery—that we may fly fastest home on broken wing.

—*William L. Sullivan*

PRAYER CONCERNS	ANSWERS
28 WEDNESDAY	1 Peter 5
29 THURSDAY	2 Peter 1
30 FRIDAY	2 Peter 2
1 SATURDAY • DECEMBER	2 Peter 3

December

I lift up my eyes to the hills—where does my help come from? My help comes from the LORD, the Maker of heaven and earth.

—Psalm 121:1–2

DECEMBER 2001

S	M	T	W	T	F	S
						1
2	3	4	5	6	7	8
9	10	11	12	13	14	15
16	17	18	19	20	21	22
23/30	24/31	25	26	27	28	29

PRAYER CONCERNS | **ANSWERS**

2 SUNDAY — 1 John 1

3 MONDAY — 1 John 2

4 TUESDAY — 1 John 3

Sorrow looks back, worry looks around, faith looks up.

—Source unknown

PRAYER CONCERNS	ANSWERS
5 WEDNESDAY	1 John 4
6 THURSDAY	1 John 5
7 FRIDAY	2 John
8 SATURDAY	3 John

Teach me to do your will, for you are my God; may your good Spirit lead me on level ground.

—Psalm 143:10

December

DECEMBER 2001						
S	M	T	W	T	F	S
						1
2	3	4	5	6	7	8
9	10	11	12	13	14	15
16	17	18	19	20	21	22
23/30	24/31	25	26	27	28	29

PRAYER CONCERNS | **ANSWERS**

9 SUNDAY — Jude

10 MONDAY — Revelation 1

11 TUESDAY — Revelation 2

I find that doing the will of God leaves me no time for disputing about His plans.

—*George MacDonald*

PRAYER CONCERNS | **ANSWERS**

12 WEDNESDAY

Revelation 3

13 THURSDAY

Revelation 4

14 FRIDAY

Revelation 5

15 SATURDAY

Revelation 6

December

The eternal God is your refuge, and underneath are the everlasting arms.

—Deuteronomy 33:27

DECEMBER 2001

S	M	T	W	T	F	S
						1
2	3	4	5	6	7	8
9	10	11	12	13	14	15
16	17	18	19	20	21	22
23/30	24/31	25	26	27	28	29

PRAYER CONCERNS	ANSWERS
16 SUNDAY	Revelation 7
17 MONDAY	Revelation 8
18 TUESDAY	Revelation 9

Live near to God by prayer. Just fall down at his feet and open your very soul before him, and throw yourself right into his arms.
—*Catherine Booth*

PRAYER CONCERNS | **ANSWERS**

19 WEDNESDAY — Revelation 10

20 THURSDAY — Revelation 11

21 FRIDAY — Revelation 12

22 SATURDAY — Revelation 13

Let us then approach the throne of grace with confidence, so that we may receive mercy and find grace to help us in our time of need.

—Hebrews 4:16

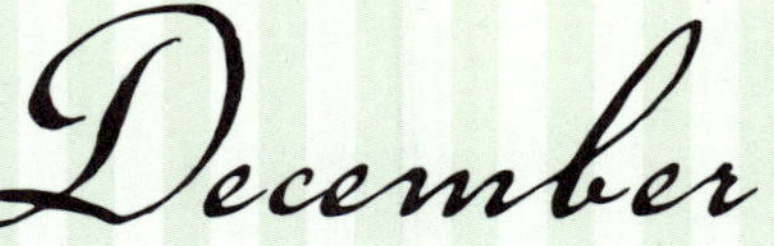

DECEMBER 2001

S	M	T	W	T	F	S
						1
2	3	4	5	6	7	8
9	10	11	12	13	14	15
16	17	18	19	20	21	22
23/30	24/31	25	26	27	28	29

PRAYER CONCERNS | **ANSWERS**

23 SUNDAY — Revelation 14

24 MONDAY — Revelation 15

25 TUESDAY — Revelation 16

We will not find God in our homes unless we stop and pray there.
—*Margaret Hebblethwaite*

PRAYER CONCERNS

ANSWERS

26 WEDNESDAY

Revelation 17

27 THURSDAY

Revelation 18

28 FRIDAY

Revelation 19

29 SATURDAY

Revelation 20

Every good and perfect gift is from above, coming down from the Father of the heavenly lights, who does not change like shifting shadows.

—James 1:17

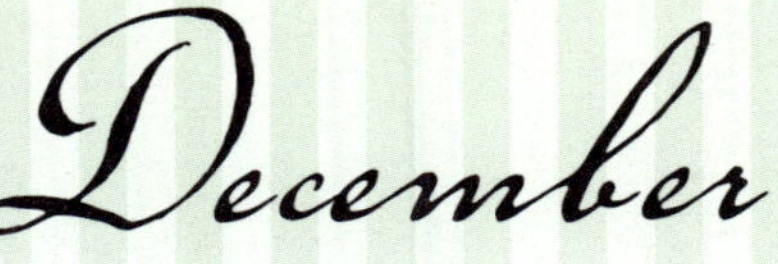

DECEMBER 2001						
S	M	T	W	T	F	S
						1
2	3	4	5	6	7	8
9	10	11	12	13	14	15
16	17	18	19	20	21	22
23/30	24/31	25	26	27	28	29

PRAYER CONCERNS	ANSWERS
30 SUNDAY	Revelation 21
31 MONDAY	Revelation 22
1 TUESDAY • JANUARY	

Our heavenly Father never takes anything from his children unless he means to give them something better.

—*George Müller*

PRAYER CONCERNS | **ANSWERS**

2 WEDNESDAY

3 THURSDAY

4 FRIDAY

5 SATURDAY

Prayer Concerns Around the World

Afghanistan

After years of civil warfare, about one-sixth of the people of **AFGHANISTAN** have either fled to other countries or are living as refugees within their own country. The nation, controlled by Muslim radicals, ranks second only to Saudi Arabia on the list of the world's worst persecutors of Christians. **PRAY** for the safety and faithfulness of the very few Christians living in Afghanistan.

Population: 25,825,000
Capital: Kabul
Language: Pushtu, Dari Persian*
Literacy: 29%
Income or GDP per capita: $800**
Religion: Muslim 99%***

Albania

In the summer of 1999, some 1,500 **ALBANIANS** made decisions for Christ during a series of showings of the *Jesus* film. This included Albanians living in Albania and also in the Kosovo region of Yugoslavia. **PRAY** for these new believers who daily face the challenges of recovering from the recent war and of dealing with economic hardship and spiritual opposition in this formerly communist nation.

Population: 3,365,000
Capital: Tiranë
Language: Albanian, Greek
Literacy: 72%
Income or GDP per capita: $1,230
Religion: Muslim 70%, Orthodox 20%, Roman Catholic 10%

*Where multiple languages are spoken, only the one or two most predominant are reported

**The per capita income figure given for most nations is actually Gross Domestic Product (GDP) per capita. In many developing nations where wealth is unevenly distributed, actual average household income may be much lower than the stated per capita GDP.

***Figures for all statistical categories are based on a comparison of several sources (see page 176) and will vary in accuracy. Percentages less than 1% are not reported.

Algeria

More than 100,000 have died since 1992 in the civil war between the government of **ALGERIA** and Muslim extremists seeking to impose Islamic law. There seems to be little hope for lasting peace until the nation can solve its serious economic problems. Christians who try to speak out for Christ often face persecution. **PRAY** for the advance of the gospel in this very difficult situation.

Population: 31,133,000
Capital: Algiers
Language: Arabic, French
Literacy: 57%
Income or GDP per capita: $4,000
Religion: Muslim 99%

Angola

As the United States and other nations drill for oil off the coast of **ANGOLA,** both sides in that nation's long civil strife use their share of the oil profits to help fund their ongoing conflict. Meanwhile the church continues to grow. **PRAY** that Christians in Angola would find ways to help end their nation's self-destruction. Pray that Western Christians, rather than seeking Angola's oil resources, would seek ways to help bring many more Angolans to Christ.

Population: 11,178,000
Capital: Luanda
Language: Bantu, Portuguese
Literacy: 42%
Income or GDP per capita: $800
Religion: Roman Catholic 69%, Protestant 20%, traditional 10%

Argentina

While the $9,700 average GDP cited below suggests that **ARGENTINA** is fairly well to do, the gap between rich and poor grows ever greater. Continent-wide, a third of all South Americans earn less than $700 per year. **PRAY** for prosperity for this part of the world. Praise God that, meanwhile, churches are growing numerically and spiritually in Argentina and elsewhere on the continent.

Population: 36,738,000
Capital: Buenos Aires
Language: Spanish, English
Literacy: 96%
Income or GDP per capita: $9,700
Religion: Roman Catholic 86%, Protestant 10%

Australia

With substantial minority groups from Asia and southern Europe, **AUSTRALIA** has great potential as a missions outpost, but most Australian Christians are nominal in their faith and lacking in missionary vision. **PRAY** for true revival in this very secularized nation. Pray for a greater concern for ministry among college students. Pray for the continued success of outreaches to the various Aboriginal people groups.

Population: 18,784,000
Capital: Canberra
Language: English
Literacy: 100%
Income or GDP per capita: $21,400
Religion: Protestant 40%, nonreligious 27%, Roman Catholic 26%, Orthodox 3%, Muslim 2%

Azerbaijan

As no less than fifty Western oil companies work feverishly to develop the rich oil reserves of **AZERBAIJAN,** most of that nation's people remain impoverished. Meanwhile there is a growing number of Christian churches, whose members are eagerly telling others of Christ despite frequent persecution. **PRAY** that many more from around the world will be drawn to Azerbaijan—to help the nation develop its *spiritual* reserves!

Population: 7,908,000
Capital: Baku
Language: Azeri
Literacy: n/a
Income or GDP per capita: $1,460
Religion: Muslim 87%,
Orthodox 11%

Though a nation of many churches, the **BAHAMAS** has been deeply affected by the materialistic and immoral influences of the tourist trade and drug trafficking. The situation could become worse as the government helps develop a gambling paradise which they expect will eventually account for 4 percent of the nation's employment and 12 percent of its economy. **PRAY** for national and church leaders who will lead in paths of righteousness.

Population: 284,000
Capital: Nassau
Language: English
Literacy: 95%
Income or GDP per capita: $19,400
Religion: Non-Anglican Protestant 50%,
Roman Catholic 26%,
Anglican 23%

Brazil

The churches of **BRAZIL** are seeking to spread the gospel both at home and abroad. One recent missions conference focused on the roughly one hundred tribes of the Amazon basin that have no Bible in their language; another conference, attended by 20,000, focused on reaching the Muslim nations of northern Africa. Praise God for the growing zeal for missions in nations such as Brazil, and **PRAY** for a rekindling of such zeal in wealthier nations such as the United States!

Population: 171,853,000
Capital: Brasília
Language: Portuguese
Literacy: 81%
Income or GDP per capita: $6,300
Religion: Roman Catholic 68%, Protestant 22%, indigenous 5%, nonreligious 2%

Bulgaria

In a climate of increasing political and religious freedom, evangelical churches in **BULGARIA** have more than doubled in size since the end of communism a decade ago. From time to time, however, there is the threat of renewed government regulation. One recent proposed law would have restricted the religious activities of those under age sixteen. **PRAY** for lasting results from a recent distribution of Bible story books to 30,000 school children.

Population: 8,195,000
Capital: Sofia
Language: Bulgarian
Literacy: 98%
Income or GDP per capita: $4,100
Religion: Orthodox 69%, nonreligious 15%, Muslim 14%, Protestant 1%

Burkina Faso

BURKINA FASO'S climate goes from encroaching desert in the north to the well-watered south, which is virtually uninhabitable because of the prevalence of disease. To cope with such challenges, the people seek to appease the spirits of their ancient animistic faith. Even Muslims in this area are really more animistic than Muslim. **PRAY** for the continuing growth and success of the many Christian ministries working in this land.

Population: 11,576,000
Capital: Ouagadougou
Language: French
Literacy: 18%
Income or GDP per capita: $950
Religion: Muslim 48%, indigenous 33%, Roman Catholic 13%, Protestant 5%

Burundi

After years of on-and-off civil warfare, many thousands of the people of **BURUNDI** have either fled to other nations or are refugees in their own land. And because tribal groups overlap national borders, civil wars in neighboring nations threaten Burundi as well. **PRAY** for a lasting solution to the chronic civil strife in this part of Africa, where the church is numerically strong on both sides of the conflict.

Population: 5,736,000
Capital: Bujumbura
Language: Kirundi, French
Literacy: 41%
Income or GDP per capita: $660
Religion: Roman Catholic 76%, Protestant 16%, indigenous 7%

Cambodia

Twenty years later, **CAMBODIA** continues to suffer the after-effects of the time when its Khmer Rouge leaders turned the nation into a "killing field," and one in seven Cambodians died. Most of its intellectual leaders died then, and its economy is still in ruins. Cambodians tend to distrust outsiders, including Christians, yet in recent years many have trusted in Christ. **PRAY** for the nearly 10,000 Cambodian believers as they live out their faith in hostile surroundings.

Population: 11,627,000
Capital: Phnom Penh
Language: Khmer, French
Literacy: 69%
Income or GDP per capita: $715
Religion: Buddhist 96%, Muslim 3%

Cameroon

Though it has been relatively prosperous in recent years, **CAMEROON** is burdened by a government that some consider the most corrupt in the world. There is religious freedom, but most Christians are nominal or even animistic in their faith and most church leaders are the products of liberal seminaries. **PRAY** for revival in the churches and seminaries.

Population: 15,456,000
Capital: Yaoundé
Language: French, English
Literacy: 54%
Income or GDP per capita: $2,100
Religion: indigenous 51%, Christian 33%, Muslim 16%

Canada

CANADIAN courts have recently begun denying tax benefits to religious workers who primarily "proselytize," while granting benefits to those engaged primarily in "social work." Meanwhile, two-thirds of all Canadians never attend church—including 1.5 million who consider themselves evangelical. **PRAY** for revival in Canada!

Population: 31,006,000
Capital: Ottawa, Ontario
Language: English, French
Literacy: 99%
Income or GDP per capita: $21,700
Religion: Roman Catholic 45%, non-Anglican Protestant 31%, Anglican 10%, nonreligious 7%, Orthodox 2%, Jewish 1%

Central African Republic

The **CENTRAL AFRICAN REPUBLIC** has been well evangelized and there are many fast-growing churches. Evangelical leaders have played key roles in helping the nation resolve political conflicts in recent years. There are many missionaries in the country, but **PRAY** for even more to help staff the dozen-plus Bible colleges that are seeking to meet the need for more and better-trained pastors.

Population: 3,445,000
Capital: Bangui
Language: French, Sangho
Literacy: 38%
Income or GDP per capita: $1,000
Religion: Protestant 47%, Roman Catholic 34%, indigenous 12%, Muslim 3%

Chad

The nation of **CHAD,** like neighboring Sudan, is divided between the Muslim north and the Christian and animistic south. There is a long history of warfare between the areas, with Muslims from the north often capturing Christians and animists and selling them as slaves. Nonetheless, Chadian Christians today are seeking to take the gospel to the Muslims. **PRAY** that peace and eternal salvation will come to all of Chad.

Population: 7,557,000
Capital: N'Djamena
Language: French, Arabic
Literacy: 30%
Income or GDP per capita: $600
Religion: Muslim 45%,
Roman Catholic 20%,
indigenous 19%, Protestant 14%

Chile

Evangelical churches have grown steadily over the past several years in **CHILE.** This has often led to fierce competition between Catholics and Protestants in terms of their differing legal status. Catholics, for instance, have traditionally had the exclusive right to provide religious education in schools. **PRAY** that all Christians in Chile would increasingly focus on evangelism and the discipleship of new believers.

Population: 14,974,000
Capital: Santiago
Language: Spanish
Literacy: 95%
Income or GDP per capita: $11,600
Religion: Roman Catholic 58%,
Protestant 28%, nonreligious 9%

People's Republic of China (mainland)

While Christianity continues to grow in the **PEOPLE'S REPUBLIC OF CHINA**, that nation also continues to persecute Christians. Meanwhile, a ministry in California saw encouraging results from a conference offering college students from China an opportunity for in-depth Bible study. **PRAY** that more and more churches and individual Christians in America will respond to opportunities to befriend and evangelize the many Chinese living among them.

Population: 1,246,872,000
Capital: Beijing
Language: Chinese
Literacy: 84%
Income or GDP per capita: $3,460
Religion: nonreligious 57%, indigenous 28%, Protestant 6%, Muslim 3%, Buddhist 3%

Republic of China (Taiwan)

While Christianity has grown rapidly among the poor and often oppressed people of mainland China, it has grown much more slowly among the free and prosperous Chinese of **TAIWAN.** Christianity has a long history in Taiwan, but is in desperate need of revival. **PRAY** that the people of Taiwan will be set free from their bondage to materialism. Pray for stronger ties between the Christians of Taiwan and those of mainland China.

Population: 22,113,000
Capital: Taipei
Language: Chinese
Literacy: 92%
Income or GDP per capita: $14,200
Religion: indigenous/ Buddhist 70%, nonreligious 24%, Protestant 3%, Roman Catholic 2%

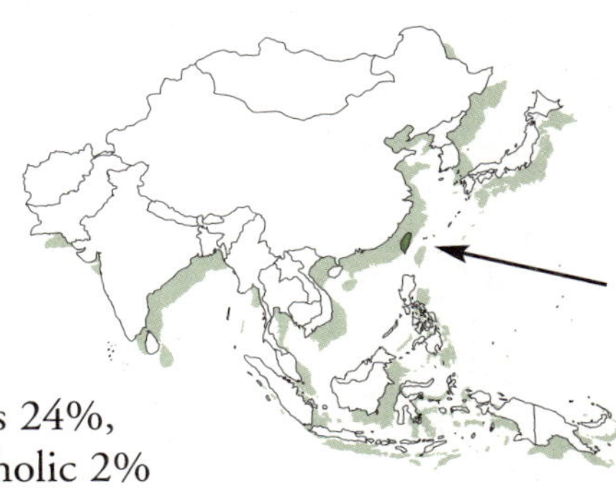

Colombia

Leftist guerrillas in **COLOMBIA** were blamed for the deaths of twenty-five evangelical pastors in the first six months of 1999, and they have forced hundreds of evangelical churches to close. Meanwhile, one village of Christian farmers destroyed hundreds of acres of opium poppies—taking a stand for their faith despite the economic sacrifice involved. **PRAY** that these brave believers will prosper and will grow ever stronger in the Lord.

Population: 39,309,000
Capital: Bogotá
Language: Spanish
Literacy: 87%
Income or GDP per capita: $6,200
Religion: Roman Catholic 93%, Protestant 5%, indigenous 1%

Congo

In many poor nations such as **CONGO,** there is a need for better medical care. Meanwhile, many medical school graduates in the United States and other Western nations want to go to such needy places but give up on their plans because of heavy debts from their years of training. **PRAY** for the continued success of one American ministry that is addressing this need by assuming responsibility for the school loans of doctors who sincerely desire to serve.

Population: 2,717,000
Capital: Brazzaville
Language: French, Lingala
Literacy: 57%
Income or GDP per capita: $2,000
Religion: Roman Catholic 50%, indigenous 23%, Protestant 22%

Democratic Republic of Congo (formerly Zaire)

Missionaries have been forced to evacuate from the **DEMOCRATIC REPUBLIC OF CONGO** three times in the past ten years, due to civil war. Yet amid the ongoing strife, church attendance has increased and local believers are carrying on many efforts begun by missionaries. **PRAY** that missionaries will be able to cope with the continual disruptions of their work; and pray for the continued faithfulness of local Christians.

Population: 50,481,000
Capital: Kinshasa
Language: French, English
Literacy: 72%
Income or GDP per capita: $400
Religion: Roman Catholic 41%, Protestant 36%, indigenous Christian 17%, indigenous 3%

While French is the official language of **CÔTE D'IVOIRE,** most of the people speak one of some seventy-five tribal languages. There are at least six languages that are spoken by less than a thousand people apiece. **PRAY** that the Lord would raise up dedicated men and women to translate the Bible into even these minor languages, so that truly people of "every nation, tribe, language and people" (Revelation 14:6) may hear the gospel.

Population: 15,818,000
Capital: Yamoussoukro
Language: French
Literacy: 54%
Income or GDP per capita: $1,700
Religion: Muslim 38%, Christian 31%, indigenous 30%

Croatia

One seminary in **CROATIA**, with 300 students, has played a key role in relief efforts and diplomatic negotiations throughout the troubled nations of former Yugoslavia. Unfortunately, however, this one seminary accounts for a large majority of the Christian workers being trained in all of this region. **PRAY** that graduates from this seminary will be able to establish similar centers for training and ministry throughout former Yugoslavia.

Population: 4,677,000
Capital: Zagreb
Language: Croatian
Literacy: 97%
Income or GDP per capita: $4,500
Religion: Roman Catholic 73%, Orthodox 14%, nonreligious 7%, Muslim 5%

A 1999 rally drew 100,000 Protestant **CUBANS** to the Plaza of the Revolution in Havana, climaxing a month of smaller celebrations in Cuba's nearly 2,000 evangelical congregations, most of which meet in homes. (A year previously, Pope John Paul II was allowed to visit the island to hold mass for Roman Catholics.) **PRAY** that Cuba's government will increasingly allow the free expression of Christian faith.

Population: 11,096,000
Capital: Havana
Language: Spanish
Literacy: 94%
Income or GDP per capita: $1,540
Religion: Roman Catholic 41%, nonreligious 31%, indigenous 24%, Protestant 3%

Denmark

DENMARK is a wealthy nation with many churches but few committed Christians. As a percentage, it sends far fewer missionaries than the other Scandinavian countries. **PRAY** for the success of the half-dozen newly established evangelical Bible schools. Pray also that more and more Danes will take an interest in reading the new Danish translation of the Bible.

Population: 5,357,000
Capital: Copenhagen
Language: Danish
Literacy: 99%
Income or GDP per capita: $23,200
Religion: Protestant 92%, nonreligious 6%, Muslim 1%

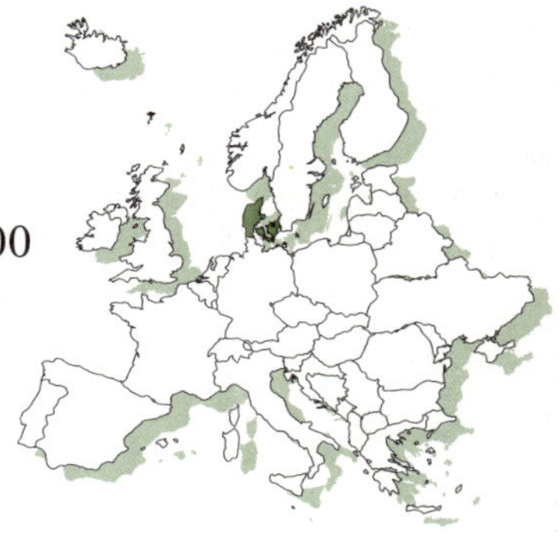

Ecuador

Some 40 percent of the people of **ECUADOR** are Amerindian, divided among two dozen language groups. In some tribes Christianity is strong, and they are sending missionaries to other nations. In other tribes, growth has stagnated because of lack of leadership and the insidious influence of materialism. **PRAY** that the glamour of the surrounding urban culture won't lure young Amerindian believers away from the truth and simplicity of the gospel.

Population: 12,562,000
Capital: Quito
Language: Spanish, Quéchua
Literacy: 90%
Income or GDP per capita: $4,400
Religion: Roman Catholic 95%, Protestant 4%

Egypt

Islamic fundamentalism has been a serious threat in recent years both to the government of **EGYPT** and to that nation's Coptic and Protestant Christians. Muslim extremists have destroyed many church buildings, and often the government refuses to allow them to be rebuilt. Meanwhile, there have been several successful evangelistic efforts, with even several Muslims coming to faith. **PRAY** for the faithful though often oppressed Christians of Egypt.

Population: 67,274,000
Capital: Cairo
Language: Arabic
Literacy: 48%
Income or GDP per capita: $4,400
Religion: Muslim 85%, Orthodox 13%, Protestant 1%

El Salvador

A conference of mayors from Central and South America highlighted the problem of domestic and other kinds of violence, often alcohol-related, as a hindrance to the continent's economic growth. For instance, they believe that violence hinders progress in **EL SALVADOR** by as much as 25 percent. **PRAY** that the fast-growing evangelical churches of El Salvador will increasingly help bring peace, prosperity, and salvation to their nation.

Population: 5,839,000
Capital: San Salvador
Language: Spanish
Literacy: 73%
Income or GDP per capita: $3,000
Religion: Roman Catholic 65%, Protestant 30%

Finland

A radio ministry based in **FINLAND** broadcasts radio and television programs in twelve languages on fifty channels throughout neighboring Russia. People responding to the programs are directed to local churches for follow-up. **PRAY** for this and the many other evangelistic outreaches of the Christians of Finland.

Population: 5,158,000
Capital: Helsinki
Language: Finnish, Swedish
Literacy: 100%
Income or GDP per capita: $20,000
Religion: Protestant 88%, nonreligious 10%, Orthodox 1%

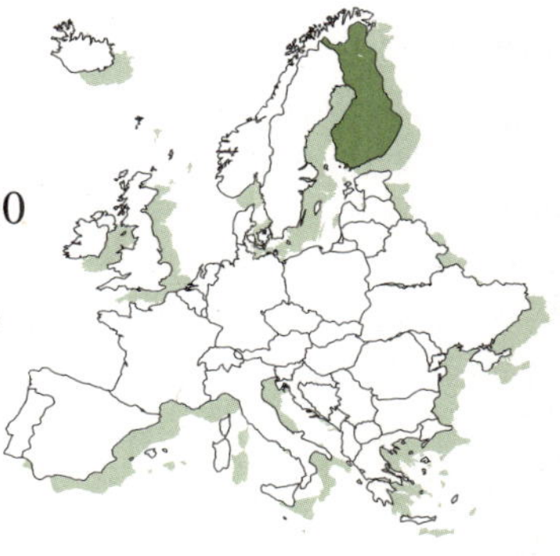

France

The government of **FRANCE** includes many evangelical groups on its list of dangerous sects. This has led to incidents of violence against such groups, as well as such things as job discrimination and even denial of banking privileges to some evangelicals. One small church recently lost its tax-exempt status and was asked to pay more than half a million dollars in back taxes. **PRAY** that the light of the gospel will not go out in France.

Population: 58,978,000
Capital: Paris
Language: French
Literacy: 99%
Income or GDP per capita: $22,700
Religion: Roman Catholic 68%, nonreligious 19%, Muslim 8%, Protestant 2%

Germany

A decade after the fall of the Berlin Wall, **GERMANY** in many ways remains divided. German churches have had little influence in former East Germany, where, after years of communist anti-Christian indoctrination, 80 percent of the people never attend church. **PRAY** for the continued faithfulness and expanding evangelistic vision of the few East German Christians whose faith actually grew stronger as a result of communist opposition.

Population: 82,087,000
Capital: Berlin
Language: German
Literacy: 99%
Income or GDP per capita:
$20,800 (average of East and West)
Religion: Protestant 37%,
Roman Catholic 36%,
nonreligious 21%, Muslim 2%

Guyana

GUYANA forsook Marxism in the early 1990s, but still suffers from a bad economy, even though it is rich in natural resources. Racially, the country is divided almost evenly between East Indians, who live mostly in rural areas, and Afro-Caribbeans, who live mainly in towns and cities. **PRAY** for ongoing efforts to reach the East Indians, who are mostly Hindu. Pray for the churches, which are deeply affected by immorality and witchcraft.

Population: 705,000
Capital: Georgetown
Language: English
Literacy: 96%
Income or GDP per capita: $2,500
Religion: Hindu 34%,
non-Anglican Protestant 18%,
Roman Catholic 18%,
Anglican 16%, Muslim 9%

Haiti

Though registered as either Protestant or Roman Catholic Christians, most of the people of **HAITI** practice voodoo as their religion, and those who stand for faith in Christ are often persecuted. The constant need for relief efforts, however, has led to a large missionary presence and many conversions to Christ. **PRAY** that these new believers will become ever stronger in their stand for the truth.

Population: 6,884,000
Capital: Port-au-Prince
Language: Creole, French
Literacy: 53%
Income or GDP per capita: $1,070
Religion: Roman Catholic 72%, Protestant 25%

Following the devastation of Hurricane Mitch in 1998, thousands of street children and other needy people from **HONDURAS** have traveled throughout Central America looking for work and housing. Too often, the children become victims of thieves or of sexual exploitation. **PRAY** for all seeking to help such people, as everyone in the region struggles to recover from the storm and from years of civil unrest.

Population: 5,997,000
Capital: Tegucigalpa
Language: Spanish
Literacy: 73%
Income or GDP per capita: $2,200
Religion: Roman Catholic 85%, Protestant 11%

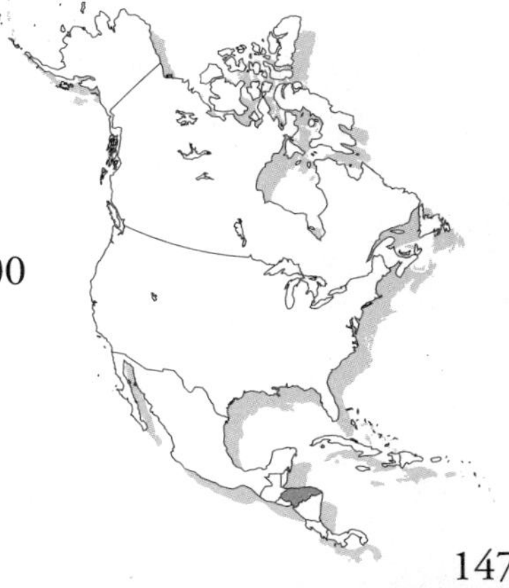

Hungary

Since the end of communist rule, many churches in **HUNGARY** have grown rapidly and have become increasingly involved in evangelism and missions. A 1998 missions conference in Budapest drew 1,400 people, with nearly 850 coming from formerly communist countries. **PRAY** that those who attended this conference will spread the flame of revival throughout Europe and Asia.

Population: 10,186,000
Capital: Budapest
Language: Hungarian
Literacy: 98%
Income or GDP per capita: $7,400
Religion: Roman Catholic 67%, Protestant 25%, nonreligious 6%, Jewish 1%

Iceland

ICELAND is financially more prosperous than ever, but still very needy spiritually, indicated by the 50 percent of births that are illegitimate. Though nearly all Icelanders belong to the Lutheran state church, only 10 percent attend regularly. **PRAY** for the few but very active evangelical churches. Pray that new evangelism resources such as the Internet would be effective in reaching this geographically isolated land.

Population: 273,000
Capital: Reykjavik
Language: Icelandic
Literacy: 100%
Income or GDP per capita: $21,000
Religion: Protestant 97%

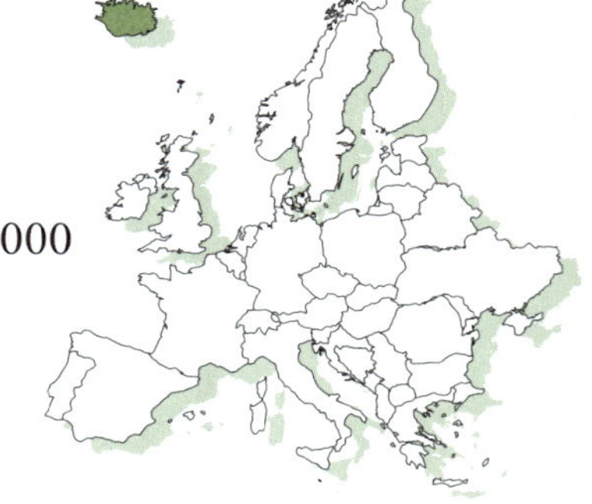

India

Recent years have seen persecution and torture of Christians who try to share the gospel with Hindus in **INDIA.** It is part of the larger struggle between those who want to maintain the nation's tradition of religious freedom and those who want to make India officially a Hindu nation. **PRAY** that the gospel will go forward in this land which is now home to more than a billion souls.

Population: 1,000,849,000
Capital: New Delhi
Language: Hindi, English
Literacy: 52%
Income or GDP per capita: $1,600
Religion: Hindu 79%, Muslim 12%, Roman Catholic 2%, Protestant 2%, Sikh 2%

Indonesia

Christianity has seen tremendous growth in mostly Muslim **INDONESIA.** Along with the growth, however, has come increasing persecution. In just one province, some 60,000 people recently lost their homes through anti-Christian violence. Despite such opposition, Christians from throughout Indonesia led the way in helping refugees from the 1999 civil strife in East Timor. **PRAY** for the safety and effective witness of these courageous believers.

Population: 216,108,000
Capital: Jakarta
Language: Indonesian
Literacy: 84%
Income or GDP per capita: $4,600
Religion: Muslim 78%, Protestant 11%, Roman Catholic 3%, Hindu 3%, Buddhist 2%

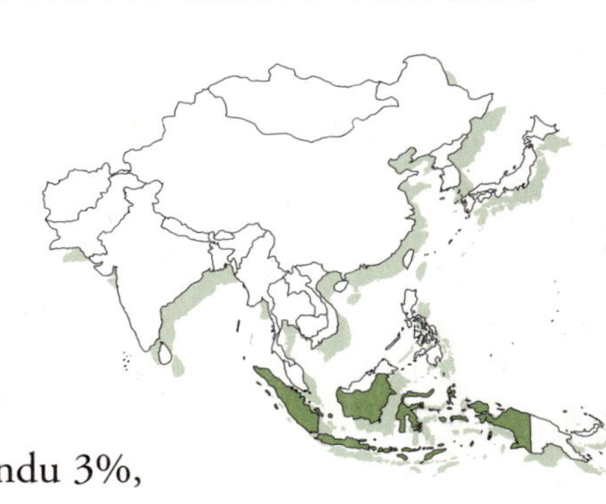

Iran

The Internet has brought a new means of evangelism to **IRAN** and other Muslim nations traditionally closed to Christian witness. **PRAY** that this powerful new tool will be a force for good, not evil. Pray that Christians from around the world will have a vision for this exciting means of reaching the lost. Pray especially for the 3.5 million Parsees of Iran, who have traditionally followed Zoroastrianism. Only thirty Parsees are known to be Christians.

Population: 65,178,000
Capital: Teheran
Language: Farsi
Literacy: 54%
Income or GDP per capita: $5,500
Religion: Muslim 98%, Orthodox 1%, Zoroastrian 1%

Iraq

While their president owns dozens of palaces, most of the people of **IRAQ** live in poverty. Life is especially difficult for the minority Kurds, whose ancestral homeland includes parts of Iraq, Iran, Turkey, Syria, and Azerbaijan. **PRAY** for the success of a Christian outreach to Kurdish women, many of whom have become prostitutes to support their families. Islam, whose founder had many wives, shows no mercy to prostitutes.

Population: 22,427,000
Capital: Baghdad
Language: Arabic
Literacy: 60%
Income or GDP per capita: $2,000
Religion: Muslim 95%, Christian 4%

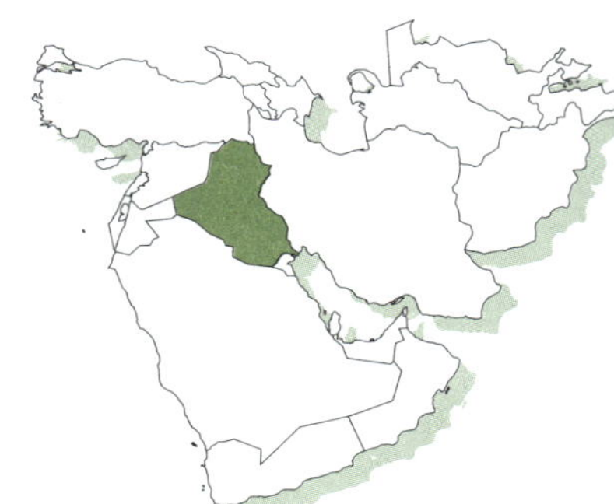

Ireland

IRELAND has become more prosperous in recent years as it has engaged more freely in world trade and become involved in high-tech industries. At the same time, it has begun liberalizing some of its laws which have traditionally upheld Christian morality. **PRAY** that Ireland will not forget God. Pray that the gospel will spread among both the Catholics and the Protestants of this nation and of Northern Ireland as well.

Population: 3,633,000
Capital: Dublin
Language: English, Irish Gaelic
Literacy: 98%
Income or GDP per capita: $18,600
Religion: Roman Catholic 94%, Anglican 4%

Recent months have seen firebombings by Orthodox Jews of both the homes and churches of Christian groups, along with rumor campaigns and attempts to pass laws restricting evangelism. Meanwhile evangelism continues, often in the form of Bible studies among Jewish and Muslim students. **PRAY** for the ongoing efforts to proclaim the gospel to all the people of Israel.

Population: 5,750,000
Capital: Jerusalem
Language: Hebrew, Arabic
Literacy: 92%
Income or GDP per capita: $17,500
Religion: Jewish 80%, Muslim 15%, Druze 2%, Roman Catholic 1%

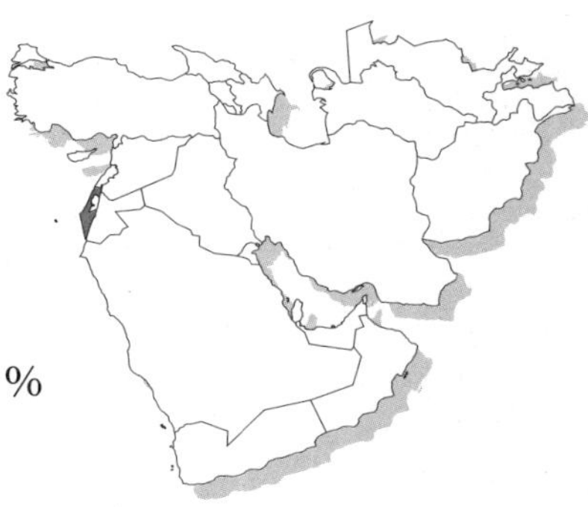

Japan

While **JAPAN** remains one of the richest nations on earth, the recession of recent years has brought an unemployment rate of 10 percent for men between 15 and 24 years of age. In 1998, an estimated ninety Japanese per day committed suicide. **PRAY** for the ongoing efforts of Japanese Christians to reach out to their friends and neighbors with the hope of salvation and eternal life.

Population: 126,182,000
Capital: Tokyo
Language: Japanese
Literacy: 99%
Income or GDP per capita: $24,500
Religion: Shinto or Buddhist 60%, indigenous 24%, nonreligious 14%, Roman Catholic 1%, Protestant 1%

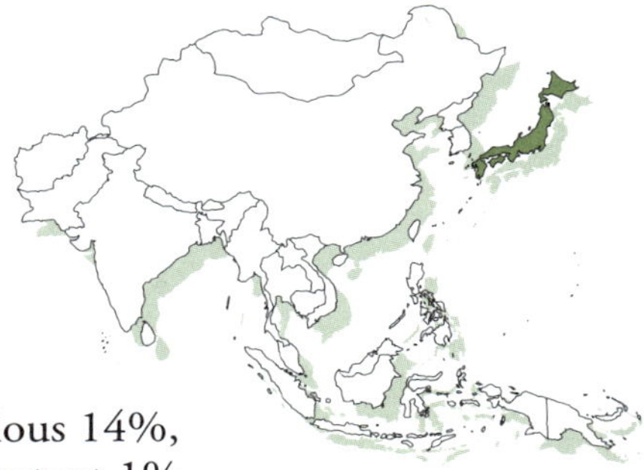

Jordan

There are several effective Christian literature ministries in **JORDAN** and other Muslim nations. One very low-key magazine seeks to address issues of spirituality and lifestyle choices. Though it has no explicit sexual content and no cigarette or tobacco ads, it is read by an estimated one-fourth of all literate youth in the Middle East! **PRAY** for the continued success of this unique outreach.

Population: 4,561,000
Capital: Amman
Language: Arabic
Literacy: 80%
Income or GDP per capita: $4,800
Religion: Muslim 94%, Orthodox 3%, Roman Catholic 2%

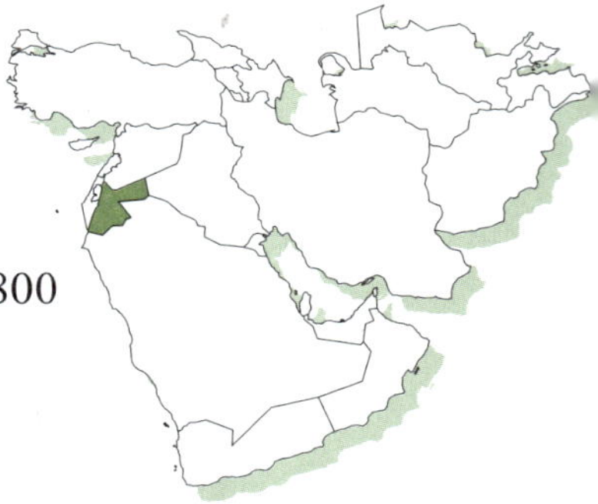

Kazakhstan

Since the end of communist rule in **KAZAKHSTAN** ten years ago, thousands of Kazakhs have returned home from other nations to which they had fled from communism. Many of these returnees face unemployment, however, in part because they no longer speak the Kazakh language. **PRAY** that the small but rapidly growing evangelical churches of Kazakhstan will reach out to these new neighbors.

Population: 16,825,000
Capital: Akmola
Language: Kazakh, Russian
Literacy: 98%
Income or GDP per capita: $3,000
Religion: Muslim 40%, nonreligious 33%, Orthodox 25%, Protestant 1%

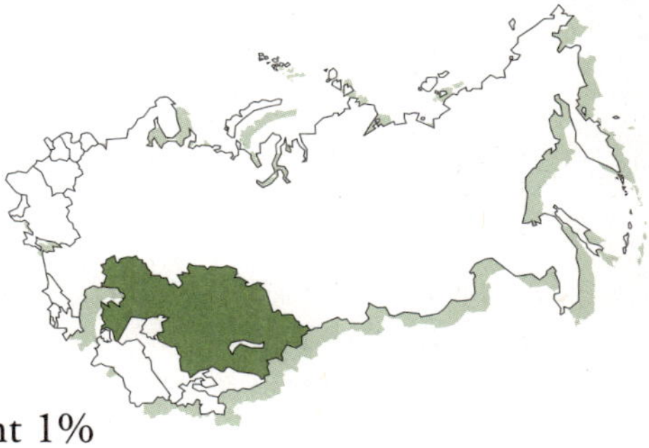

Korea (North)

Floods, droughts, and economic mismanagement have caused at least 2 million deaths from famine in **NORTH KOREA** since 1995. Some 70 percent of children under five years of age are still in danger of dying. **PRAY** for the ongoing efforts of international relief agencies, of South Korean Christians, and of the South Korean government to reach out to North Korea in this time of desperate need.

Population: 21,386,000
Capital: Pyongyang
Language: Korean
Literacy: 100%
Income or GDP per capita: $900
Religion: nonreligious 67%, indigenous 29%, Buddhist 2%, Christian 1%

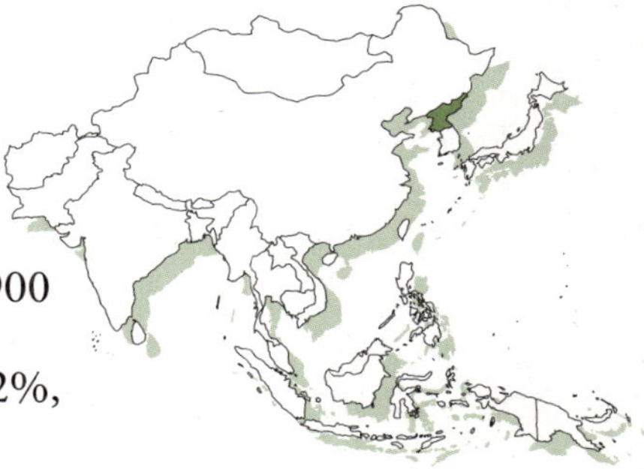

Korea (South)

The fast-growing Christian churches of **SOUTH KOREA** have for many years been a significant force in world missions. The recent economic recession in Asia has been a challenge as missions giving declined. It has also highlighted the spiritual darkness of the region, as many formerly well-to-do Koreans abandoned their children because of their new hardships. **PRAY** for the faithfulness and effective ministry of the churches of South Korea.

Population: 46,885,000
Capital: Seoul
Language: Korean
Literacy: 98%
Income or GDP per capita: $13,700
Religion: Buddhist 33%, indigenous 24%, indigenous Christian 14%, Confucian 12%, Protestant 12%, Roman Catholic 4%

Kuwait

While **KUWAIT** remains predominantly Muslim, there are a growing number of Christians among those from other nations who have come there to work in the oil industry. One church has an average weekly attendance of 15,000, representing forty-two nationalities! **PRAY** that this church will continue to prosper and that its members will reflect the love of Christ as they go about their daily work in Kuwait.

Population: 1,991,000
Capital: Kuwait
Language: Arabic, English
Literacy: 73%
Income or GDP per capita: $22,300
Religion: Muslim 95%, Roman Catholic 2%

Laos

The years during and after the Vietnam War saw a massive flow of refugees from **LAOS** and the other nations of Southeast Asia. Many of these refugees settled in the United States, Canada, and Europe. Some have become Christians and some of these are now returning to their homelands as missionaries. **PRAY** for the success of this exciting new trend in world missions.

Population: 5,407,000
Capital: Vientiane
Language: Lao, French
Literacy: 45%
Income or GDP per capita: $1,150
Religion: Buddhist 84%, animist 14%, Christian 1%

Latvia

Delegates from **LATVIA** recently traveled to Moscow to take part in a conference of Christian broadcasters from across the former Soviet Union. The Latvian government is encouraging efforts to reverse the effects of years of communist indoctrination; it is even calling for a return of religious education in public schools. **PRAY** that the church in Latvia will take full advantage of the current opportunities to turn their nation back to Christ.

Population: 2,354,000
Capital: Riga
Language: Latvian
Literacy: 100%
Income or GDP per capita: $4,260
Religion: nonreligious 44%, Roman Catholic 20%, Protestant 20%, Orthodox 15%

Liberia

Out of the devastation of the recent civil war in **LIBERIA** has come a home-grown missionary agency, founded by a former street child, which has built several orphanages and a Bible college and has helped establish more than 200 churches throughout Liberia and surrounding nations. **PRAY** for the continued success of this vital ministry, and pray for a lasting peace in Liberia.

Population: 2,924,000
Capital: Monrovia
Language: English
Literacy: 40%
Income or GDP per capita: $1,000
Religion: indigenous 62%, Protestant 21%, Muslim 13%, Roman Catholic 3%

Libya

In power since 1969, **LIBYA'S** Muammar Qaddhafi has sought to make his nation the center of a united Arab world. He has promoted Islam and has tried to rid Africa of the influence of colonialism and Christianity. Christian witness has been nearly impossible during this time, but there have been recent signs that Qaddhafi may be softening his policy. **PRAY** for all efforts to proclaim the gospel in Libya.

Population: 4,993,000
Capital: Tripoli
Language: Arabic, Italian
Literacy: 64%
Income or GDP per capita: $6,700
Religion: Muslim 96%, Orthodox 2%, Roman Catholic 1%

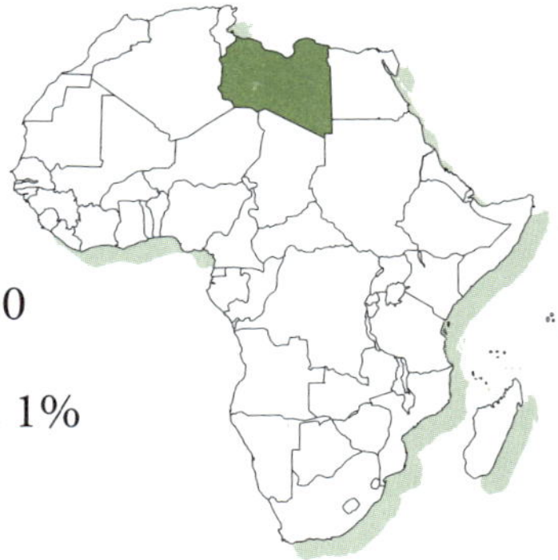

Macedonia

A nation of only 2 million which for a long time avoided the conflict in former Yugoslavia, **MACEDONIA** has in recent months seen an "invasion" of hundreds of thousands of mostly Muslim refugees from the fighting in Kosovo. **PRAY** for lasting fruit of the efforts of international Christian relief workers to minister to these refugees and to present the gospel to them. Pray that the regional conflict will not engulf Macedonia as well.

Population: 2,023,000
Capital: Skopje
Language: Macedonian, Albanian
Literacy: 85%
Income or GDP per capita: $960
Religion: Orthodox 60%,
Muslim 26%, nonreligious 11%

Madagascar

The Christian churches of **MADAGASCAR** have a long and proud history of growing strong amid persecution. Today, however, there is a need for revival. **PRAY** that the recent successes of youth ministries will continue. Pray for an increased interest in cross-cultural missions; Malagasy believers tend to be isolated by geography, language, and a lack of financial resources.

Population: 14,873,000
Capital: Antananarivo
Language: Malagasy, French
Literacy: 80%
Income or GDP per capita: $730
Religion: indigenous 52%,
Christian 41%, Muslim 7%

Malawi

Christian churches are growing stronger in **MALAWI**, but they face serious challenges. Islam is also on the increase, with the help of Mideastern oil money. And 27 percent of children under age fifteen are orphans, largely because of the AIDS epidemic. **PRAY** that the church in Malawi will rise to meet these challenges, and will grow in zeal for proclaiming the gospel at home and in the other nations of southern Africa.

Population: 10,000,000
Capital: Lilongwe
Language: English, Chichewa
Literacy: 49%
Income or GDP per capita: $900
Religion: Protestant 35%, Roman Catholic 26%, indigenous 23%, Muslim 14%

Mali

Though officially Muslim, the desert nation of **MALI** is wide open to Christian evangelization. Many came to Christ as a result of famine relief by Christian groups in the early 1980s. But both Christians and Muslims are likely to be drawn into the pervasive world of traditional spirit worship. **PRAY** for missionaries and for mature local church leaders to respond to this unique opportunity to take the gospel to Muslims.

Population: 10,429,000
Capital: Bamako
Language: French
Literacy: 32%
Income or GDP per capita: $600
Religion: Muslim 86%, indigenous 11%, Roman Catholic 2%

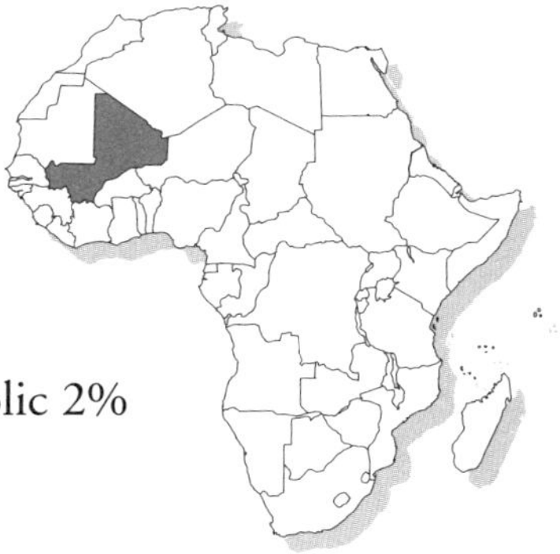

Marshall Islands

Any income earned by the people of the **MARSHALL ISLANDS** is rendered almost meaningless by the amount of foreign aid and compensation they receive from the United States for the lingering effects of the atomic bombs tested on Bikini and Eniwetok during World War II. As a result, drunkenness, drugs, materialism, and lack of motivation are chronic problems. **PRAY** for the churches as they address these problems.

Population: 66,000
Capital: Majuro
Language: Marshallese, English
Literacy: 91%
Income or GDP per capita: $1,680
Religion: Protestant 80%, Roman Catholic 10%, animist 4%, nonreligious 2%

Mauritania

Covered mostly by the Sahara desert, **MAURITANIA** is possibly the most nomadic nation on earth, with 80 percent of its people making their living from herding cattle and sheep. Christian evangelism is nearly impossible in this Muslim nation. **PRAY** that Christians working with economic development organizations in the area will find opportunities for sharing their faith.

Population: 2,582,000
Capital: Nouakchott
Language: Arabic, French
Literacy: 34%
Income or GDP per capita: $1,750
Religion: Muslim 99%

Mexico

A missionary organization founded by **MEXICAN** nationals has formed a missionary training center in Mexico City. Meanwhile, within Mexico itself there's a growing nationwide effort to establish thousands of home churches. **PRAY** for the spiritual and physical well-being of the Mexican people. While NAFTA has brought greater prosperity to some, especially in the north, most Mexicans are worse off today than they were five years ago.

Population: 100,294,000
Capital: Mexico City
Language: Spanish
Literacy: 87%
Income or GDP per capita: $7,700
Religion: Roman Catholic 88%, Protestant 6%, nonreligious 4%

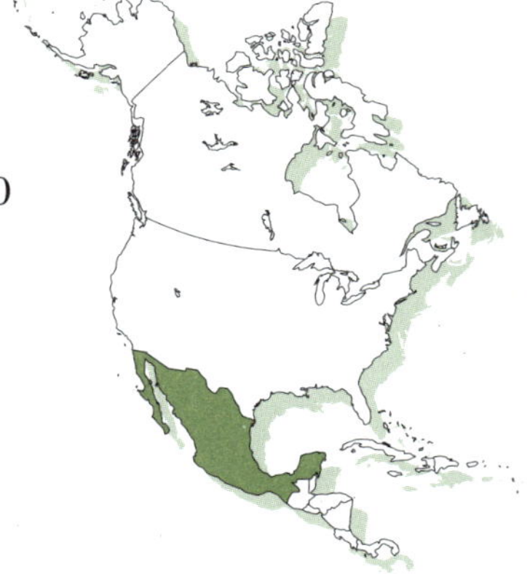

Morocco

Though its beaches and bazaars are a popular destination for European tourists, **MOROCCO** is a solidly Muslim nation where Christian witness can land one in jail. Recent years, however, have brought some signs of liberalization, as the nation has sought a balance between the forces of Islam and its desire for European economic investment. **PRAY** that changing times in Morocco will open doors for the gospel.

Population: 29,662,000
Capital: Rabat
Language: Arabic, French
Literacy: 50%
Income or GDP per capita: $3,500
Religion: Muslim 99%

Namibia

As is true of many other nations in sub-Saharan Africa, nearly a fourth of **NAMIBIA's** adults are HIV-positive. That leads to other problems as well, such as a growing number of orphans, lack of medical care for other ailments, and a general decrease in living standards. **PRAY** that Namibia's church leaders and government officials will increasingly work together to address the moral problems at the root of the AIDS epidemic.

Population: 1,648,000
Capital: Windhoek
Language: Afrikaans, German
Literacy: 38%
Income or GDP per capita: $3,700
Religion: Protestant 68%,
Roman Catholic 16%, indigenous
Christian 7%, nonreligious 4%

New Zealand

Even as **NEW ZEALAND** becomes more wealthy and secularized, there is significant growth among evangelical churches. There are nearly two dozen good Bible colleges, and on a per capita basis New Zealand sends nearly as many missionaries as the United States. **PRAY** for continued revival. Pray that Christian churches will be seen as places where New Zealanders of European, Polynesian, and other ancestries work together as brothers and sisters.

Population: 3,662,000
Capital: Wellington
Language: English, Maori
Literacy: 99%
Income or GDP per capita: $17,700
Religion: Protestant 50%,
nonreligious 29%,
Roman Catholic 15%

Nicaragua

In **NICARAGUA** as in the rest of Central America, evangelical churches have grown rapidly in recent years. Yet problems persist, as 70 percent of pastors have had no formal training, and 60 percent of the region's people live in poverty. **PRAY** for the success of the many local Christian groups seeking to address both the economic and the spiritual challenges all around them.

Population: 4,717,000
Capital: Managua
Language: Spanish
Literacy: 57%
Income or GDP per capita: $2,100
Religion: Roman Catholic 75%,
Protestant 20%

Pakistan

While the GDP figures for **PAKISTAN** (see below) indicate an average per capita income of $2,600, nearly a third of the people earn less than a dollar a day. Efforts of Christian groups to help out with the resulting needs are often hampered by opposition from Muslim extremists. **PRAY** for greater opportunities for Pakistani Christians and Christians from other nations to reach out to the people of Pakistan.

Population: 138,123,000
Capital: Islamabad
Language: Urdu, English
Literacy: 35%
Income or GDP per capita: $2,600
Religion: Muslim 95%,
Hindu 2%, Christian 2%

Panama

As control of the canal is transferred from the United States to **PANAMA**, many fear that drug runners from South America will use the transition as an opportunity to increasingly use Panamanian territory as a base for their trade. **PRAY** for Panama as it faces this challenge. Pray that the gospel will bring eternal salvation to many Panamanians, and renewed morality and prosperity to the nation.

Population: 2,779,000
Capital: Panama City
Language: Spanish
Literacy: 89%
Income or GDP per capita: $6,700
Religion: Roman Catholic 73%, Protestant 17%, Muslim 5%

Paraguay

Evangelical Christianity has grown very slowly in **PARAGUAY** until just the past twenty years, when there have been several successful evangelistic crusades. Today there is an open door for missionaries, and many are needed, especially among college students. **PRAY** also for Bible translators, and for people to be involved in the distribution of Bibles and Christian literature.

Population: 5,434,000
Capital: Asunción
Language: Spanish, Guaraní
Literacy: 90%
Income or GDP per capita: $3,900
Religion: Roman Catholic 92%, Protestant 6%

Peru

Although it has had relative peace for the past few years, **PERU** still suffers the after-effects of many years of civil warfare. Of special concern are the more than 100,000 children who are homeless and more than 50,000 orphans. **PRAY** that those in Peru who openly claim Christ as their Savior will set an example in caring for the needs of these children.

Population: 26,625,000
Capital: Lima
Language: Spanish, Quéchua
Literacy: 85%
Income or GDP per capita: $4,420
Religion: Roman Catholic 89%, Protestant 7%

Poland

The Roman Catholic Church successfully preserved **POLAND** as a Christian nation throughout its many years of domination by the Soviet Union. Having broken its Soviet ties during the 1980s, Poland reached another post-communism milestone in 1999 as it became a member of NATO. **PRAY** that in this third Christian millennium more and more Poles will find a personal faith in Christ.

Population: 38,609,000
Capital: Warsaw
Language: Polish
Literacy: 98%
Income or GDP per capita: $7,250
Religion: Roman Catholic 88%, nonreligious 10%, Orthodox 1%, Protestant 1%

Russia

While **RUSSIA** struggles politically and economically, there are signs of renewed interest in Christianity throughout the nation. In addition to the Christian broadcasts from Finland (see prayer concern for that country), another radio ministry reaches an estimated 17 percent of all Russians weekly. **PRAY** for a great return to Christ throughout Russia, and for the health and prosperity of the nation.

Population: 146,394,000
Capital: Moscow
Language: Russian
Literacy: 98%
Income or GDP per capita: $4,700
Religion: Orthodox 55%, nonreligious 33%, Muslim 9%

Senegal

SENEGAL has a strong tradition of religious freedom compared to other Muslim nations. Yet among the approximately three million people of the Wolof tribe—one-third of the nation—there are only a few hundred Christians. Finally, however, the New Testament is available in their language. **PRAY** that many of the Wolof people will learn to read, and that their first book will be God's Word!

Population: 10,052,000
Capital: Dakar
Language: French, Wolof
Literacy: 38%
Income or GDP per capita: $1,850
Religion: Muslim 92%, indigenous 6%, Christian 2%

Singapore

As part of its effort to recover from the Asian economic recession, **SINGAPORE** is becoming more open to Western ideas and is sending more of its people abroad for business and schooling. **PRAY** that this will mean even greater opportunities for the gospel in this tiny nation that is so influential throughout all of Asia, and is home to several international Christian ministries.

Population: 3,532,000
Capital: Singapore
Language: Malay, Chinese
Literacy: 90%
Income or GDP per capita: $24,600
Religion: Buddhist or Taoist 52%, Muslim 15%, nonreligious 14%, Protestant 8%, Roman Catholic 6%, Hindu 3%

Slovakia

The Gypsies of **SLOVAKIA,** forced under communism to leave their nomadic ways and take jobs in factories, are now largely unemployed, live in shanty towns, and are rejected by their neighbors. But many have responded to a Christian ministry which has established schools for their children and vocational training for adults, while also sharing the gospel. **PRAY** that these wanderers will find a permanent home—in Christ.

Population: 5,396,000
Capital: Bratislava
Language: Slovak
Literacy: 99%
Income or GDP per capita: $8,600
Religion: Roman Catholic 60%, nonreligious 25%, Protestant 15%

Slovenia

SLOVENIA is the most ethnically and religiously homogenous of the former republics of Yugoslavia, and has suffered the least from the warfare in that region. **PRAY** that knowledge of the gospel will flourish in this setting, and that Slovenia will remain an island of calm in this part of the world while reaching out to those in the more troubled areas.

Population: 1,971,000
Capital: Ljubljana
Language: Slovenian, Serbo-Croatian
Literacy: 99%
Income or GDP per capita: $10,000
Religion: Roman Catholic 81%, nonreligious 17%, Protestant 1%

Somalia

For its entry on **SOMALIA** under the heading of "government," *Time Almanac 2000* listed "none"; Somalia has had no official government since 1991. As a result of that instability and chronic famine, many Somalians eat only one meal per day. Somalia does, however, excel in one area: It ranks as the world's fourth leading persecutor of Christians. **PRAY** for openings for presenting the gospel in this very difficult and dangerous area.

Population: 7,141,000
Capital: Mogadishu
Language: Somali, Arabic
Literacy: 24%
Income or GDP per capita: $600
Religion: Muslim 99%

South Africa

As **SOUTH AFRICA** continues its long journey beyond racial separatism, many challenges remain. Evangelical Christians were instrumental in ending apartheid and continue to play a key role in the process of national healing. **PRAY** that the Christians of South Africa will persevere in addressing the issues of reconciliation, and that they will also seek to reconcile all South Africans to their heavenly Father (2 Corinthians 5:11–21).

Population: 43,426,000
Capital: Pretoria
Language: English, Afrikaans
Literacy: 76%
Income or GDP per capita: $6,200
Religion: non-Anglican Protestant 39%, indigenous Christian 22%, indigenous 16%, Roman Catholic 10%, Anglican 7%, Hindu 2%

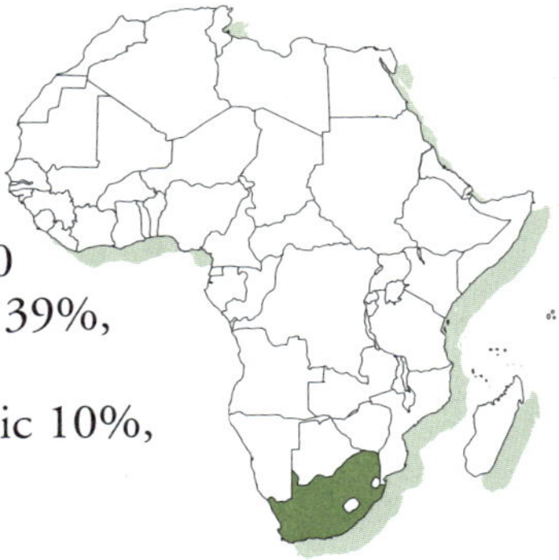

Sudan

For years, Christians in **SUDAN** have been persecuted by their Islamic-led government. Some 4 million have been either enslaved or displaced from their homes. One result of this upheaval has been rapid church growth. **PRAY** for good leadership for these new believers. Pray also for wisdom on the part of international Christian groups seeking to buy Sudanese Christians out of slavery. Some feel that these well-meaning efforts only make matters worse.

Population: 34,476,000
Capital: Khartoum
Language: Arabic, English
Literacy: 27%
Income or GDP per capita: $875
Religion: Muslim 70%, Christian 19%, indigenous 9%

Sweden

Though it has been known in recent years for its liberal politics and lax morality, there is a solid bedrock of evangelical Christianity in **SWEDEN,** and Swedes are still a substantial force in world missions. **PRAY** that the new, modern-language *Swedish People's Bible* will bring revival to the church and culture of Sweden.

Population: 8,911,000
Capital: Stockholm
Language: Swedish
Literacy: 99%
Income or GDP per capita: $19,700
Religion: Protestant 60%, nonreligious 35%, Roman Catholic 2%, Orthodox 1%

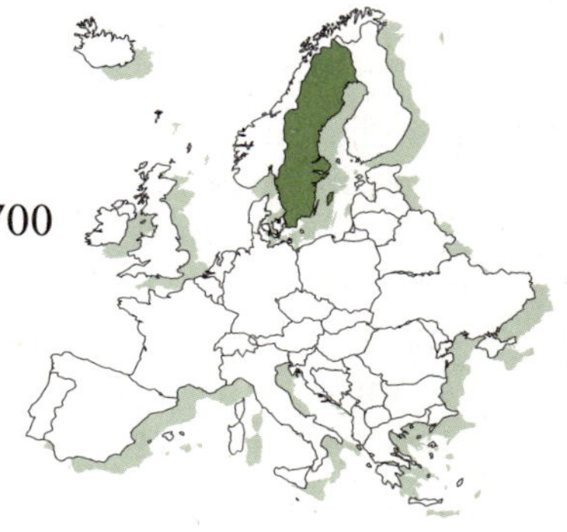

Tanzania

Hunger has been a problem in **TANZANIA** in recent years, and many have responded to the gospel as a result of famine relief efforts by American Christians. Actually, on a worldwide basis, the number of famine victims has declined in recent years, thanks to the return of prosperity and democracy to many regions, and to the efforts of Western relief agencies. **PRAY** that Christians will never forget the needs of the world's poor.

Population: 31,271,000
Capital: Dar es Salaam
Language: Swahili, English
Literacy: 52%
Income or GDP per capita: $700
Religion: Muslim 35%, Roman Catholic 31%, Protestant 19%, animist 13%

Turkey

In 1999 the government of mostly Muslim **TURKEY** prohibited the opening of a Christian church camp; shortly thereafter, Christians were using the campsite to house earthquake survivors. Nonetheless, Christians in Turkey have continued to suffer persecution, with churches being raided and those in attendance jailed. **PRAY** that those in Turkey who favor religious tolerance will win out over those favoring Islamic law.

Population: 65,599,000
Capital: Ankara
Language: Turkish
Literacy: 81%
Income or GDP per capita: $6,100
Religion: Muslim 99%

Turkmenistan

After allowing religious freedom for several years, the formerly Soviet nation of **TURKMENISTAN** passed a law in 1996 stating that a religious organization must have at least 500 members to be legal (most evangelical groups are much smaller than that). Undaunted by this challenge, in 1998 thirteen Turkmen Christians traveled some 4,000 miles by bus to attend a missions conference in Hungary. **PRAY** for God's richest blessings on these zealous ambassadors for Christ.

Population: 4,366,000
Capital: Ashgabat
Language: Turkmen
Literacy: 98%
Income or GDP per capita: $3,000
Religion: Muslim 76%, nonreligious 18%, Orthodox 5%

Uganda

The AIDS epidemic and recurrent civil war in **UGANDA** has given birth to many home-grown Christian ministries. In one town of 30,000, a school established for the orphans of AIDS victims has grown to accommodate many other students as well; it is the only school in town. **PRAY** for this school as it seeks also to establish a medical clinic and a college for teacher training and Bible instruction.

Population: 22,805,000
Capital: Kampala
Language: English, Swahili
Literacy: 54%
Income or GDP per capita: $1,700
Religion: Roman Catholic 42%,
Protestant 30%, tribal 11%,
Muslim 7%, indigenous 6%, Baha'i 3%

United Kingdom

Though it has played a key role in the history of the church, the **UNITED KINGDOM** (England, Scotland, Wales, and Northern Ireland) has become increasingly secularized in recent years. A 1990 law, for instance, denied the right of any religious group to own a radio license, thus restricting religious programming to the state-owned BBC. **PRAY** for a revival that will reach the UK and all the nations worldwide where its influence is felt.

Population: 59,113,000
Capital: London
Language: English
Literacy: 99%
Income or GDP per capita: $21,200
Religion: Anglican 50%,
nonreligious 26%,
non-Anglican Protestant 10%,
Roman Catholic 9%,
Muslim 3%, Jewish 1%

United States

According to one survey, thirty years ago some 15 percent of teens in the **UNITED STATES OF AMERICA** identified themselves as evangelical Christians, but today that number has shrunk to just 4 percent! **PRAY** that the church in America would seek to reach the nation's youth. Pray for stronger families. Pray that the Internet, rather than luring young people away from Christ, would become a powerful means of evangelism in America and around the world.

Population: 272,878,000
Capital: Washington, D.C.
Language: English
Literacy: 97%
Income or GDP per capita: $30,200
Religion: Protestant 56%,
Roman Catholic 28%,
nonreligious 7%, Jewish 3%,
Orthodox 3%, Muslim 2%

Uruguay

Traditionally a very secularized nation, **URUGUAY** has been the scene in recent years of a unique Christian outreach: Sixty or so of the capital city's 3,000 taxi drivers have formed the Christian Taxi Driver Association, witnessing to their passengers from all levels of society at all hours of the day and night. **PRAY** for the continued success of these "evangelists on wheels." Pray that their vision will spread to taxi drivers in other nations.

Population: 3,309,000
Capital: Montevideo
Language: Spanish
Literacy: 96%
Income or GDP per capita: $8,900
Religion: Roman Catholic 48%,
nonreligious 37%,
Protestant 4%, Jewish 2%

Uzbekistan

In **UZBEKISTAN**, four Muslim converts to Christianity were sentenced to long prison terms on false charges. One of the men led ninety-five fellow prisoners to Christ while in prison awaiting trial! **PRAY** for these ninety-five new believers as they begin their Christian life in a part of the world where there are few opportunities for Bible teaching or Christian fellowship.

Population: 24,102,000
Capital: Tashkent
Language: Uzbek, Russian
Literacy: 97%
Income or GDP per capita: $2,500
Religion: Muslim 68%, nonreligious 26%, Orthodox 4%

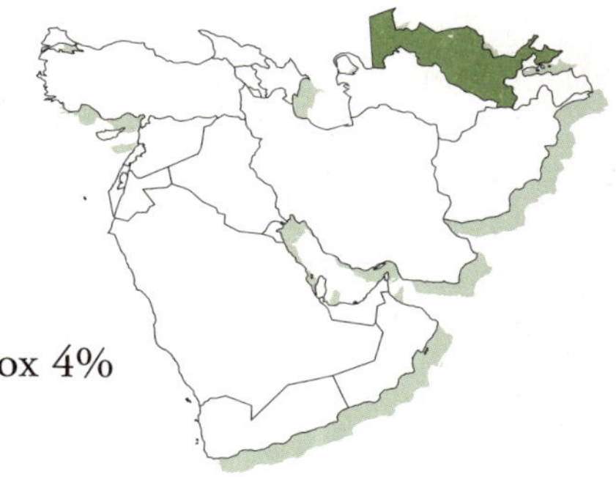

Venezuela

Evangelical churches have grown steadily in **VENEZUELA** over the past few years, and many believers have sought to become more active in their nation's public life. **PRAY** that these Christians will be a force for good in addressing problems such as widespread immorality, the many problems associated with drug trafficking, and the corruption that has allowed only those with political power to benefit from the nation's oil wealth.

Population: 23,203,000
Capital: Caracas
Language: Spanish
Literacy: 91%
Income or GDP per capita: $8,300
Religion: Roman Catholic 88%, Protestant 5%, nonreligious 2%, animist 2%

Yugoslavia (Serbia and Montenegro)

As the nations and people groups formerly comprising **YUGOSLAVIA** continue to break apart, hundreds of thousands in that region live as refugees in their own land or in neighboring nations. **PRAY** that, as relief workers share Christ with both Muslims and nominally Orthodox Christians, centuries of bitter rivalry will be left at the foot of the cross. Pray especially for the children of this troubled area.

Population: 11,207,000
Capital: Belgrade
Language: Serbo-Croatian
Literacy: 91%
Income or GDP per capita: $2,280
Religion: Orthodox 67%,
Muslim 17%, nonreligious 9%,
Catholic 6%

Zambia

Despite the well-established influence of Christianity in **ZAMBIA,** nearly a fourth of its adult population is HIV-positive. Of the thirty-three million people worldwide infected with the HIV virus, two-thirds live in Africa. **PRAY** for the many churches of Zambia that are making renewed efforts to teach Christian morality to their members and to evangelize nonbelievers.

Population: 9,664,000
Capital: Lusaka
Language: English
Literacy: 73%
Income or GDP per capita: $950
Religion: Roman Catholic 32%,
indigenous 32%, Protestant 27%

Remember these other nations . . .

The worldwide family of nations is nearly 200-strong. Space allows the inclusion of only about half of those nations in this volume. The following were not included, but deserve a place in our prayers.

Andorra
Antigua and Barbuda
Armenia
Austria
Bahrain
Bangladesh
Barbados
Belarus
Belgium
Belize
Benin
Bhutan
Bolivia
Bosnia and Herzegovina
Botswana
Brunei Darussalam
Cape Verde
Comoros
Costa Rica
Cyprus
Czech Republic
Djibouti
Dominica
Dominican Republic
Equatorial Guinea
Eritrea
Estonia
Ethiopia
Fiji
Gabon
Gambia
Georgia
Ghana
Greece
Grenada
Guatemala
Guinea
Guinea-Bissau
Italy
Jamaica
Kenya
Kiribati
Kyrgyzstan
Lebanon
Lesotho
Liechtenstein
Lithuania
Luxembourg
Malaysia
Maldives
Malta
Mauritius
Micronesia
Moldova
Monaco
Mongolia
Mozambique
Myanmar (formerly Burma)
Nauru
Nepal
Netherlands
Niger
Nigeria
Norway
Oman
Palau
Papua New Guinea
Philippines
Portugal
Qatar
Romania
Rwanda
Samoa
San Marino
São Tomé and Príncipe
Saudi Arabia
Seychelles
Sierra Leone
Solomon Islands
Spain
Sri Lanka
St. Kitts and Nevis
St. Lucia
St. Vincent and Grenadines
Suriname
Swaziland
Switzerland
Syria
Tajikistan
Thailand
Togo
Tonga
Trinidad and Tobago
Tunisia
Tuvalu
Ukraine
United Arab Emirates
Vanuatu
Vatican City State
Vietnam
Western Sahara
Yemen
Zimbabwe

Sources

Christianity Today.

Charles Noel Douglas, comp., *Forty Thousand Quotations* (New York: Halcyon, 1917).

Patrick Johnstone, *Operation World* (Grand Rapids, Mich.: Zondervan, 1993).

The New Dictionary of Thoughts (New York: Doubleday, 1977).

George Otis, Jr., ed., *Strongholds of the 10/40 Window* (Seattle, Wash.: YWAM, 1995).

Pulse newsletter (published by Evangelism and Missions Information Service of the Billy Graham Center at Wheaton College, P.O. Box 794, Wheaton, IL 60189).

Reader's Digest

The Time Almanac 2000 (Boston: Information Please LCC, 1999).

U.S. News and World Report.

Hannah Ward and Jennifer Wild, *The Doubleday Christian Quotation Collection* (New York: Doubleday, 1997).

Albert M. Wells, Jr., comp., *Inspiring Quotations* (Nashville: Thomas Nelson, 1988).